Routledge Revivals

Investigating Rape

First published in 1985, *Investigating Rape* examines practices related with rape in four United States police departments and suggests what lessons the British police service might draw from them. The author urges greater recognition of the emotional trauma suffered by rape victims and the effects of that trauma on the relationship between victims and investigators. He recommends changes in police procedure, including new approaches in interviewing style and changes in training and in liaison with agencies who provide help to victims. This book will be of interest to any police official as well as to students of law and criminology.

Investigating Rape

A new approach for police

Ian Blair

First published in 1985
By Croom Helm Ltd.

This edition first published in 2024 by Routledge
4 Park Square, Milton Park, Abingdon, Oxon, OX14 4RN
and by Routledge
605 Third Avenue, New York, NY 10017

Routledge is an imprint of the Taylor & Francis Group, an informa business

© 1985 Ian Blair

All rights reserved. No part of this book may be reprinted or reproduced or utilised in any form or by any electronic, mechanical, or other means, now known or hereafter invented, including photocopying and recording, or in any information storage or retrieval system, without permission in writing from the publishers.

Publisher's Note
The publisher has gone to great lengths to ensure the quality of this reprint but points out that some imperfections in the original copies may be apparent.

Disclaimer
The publisher has made every effort to trace copyright holders and welcomes correspondence from those they have been unable to contact.

A Library of Congress record exists under ISBN: 0709920989

ISBN: 978-1-032-74595-4 (hbk)
ISBN: 978-1-003-47000-7 (ebk)
ISBN: 978-1-032-74596-1 (pbk)

Book DOI 10.4324/9781003470007

Investigating Rape:

A new approach for police

Ian Blair

CROOM HELM
London • Sydney • Dover, New Hampshire

In association with
THE POLICE FOUNDATION

© 1985 Ian Blair
Croom Helm Ltd, Provident House, Burrell Row,
Beckenham, Kent BR3 1AT
Croom Helm Australia Pty Ltd, First Floor, 139 King Street,
Sydney, NSW 2001, Australia

British Library Cataloguing in Publication Data

Investigating rape: a new approach for police.
 1. Rape——Investigation
 I. Blair, Ian
 364.1'532   HV8079.R35

ISBN 0-7099-2098-9

Croom Helm Ltd, 51 Washington St.,
Dover, New Hampshire 03820

Library of Congress Cataloging in Publication Data

Blair, Ian, 1953–
  Investigating rape

  Bibliography: p. 103.
  Includes index.
  1. Rape—Great Britain—Investigation. 2. Rape—
United States—Investigation. I. Title.
HV8079.R35B55   1985   363.2'5   84–23802
ISBN 0–7099–2098–9

Printed and bound in Great Britain

CONTENTS

List of tables and figures
Foreword
Acknowledgements
Preface   1

1 Introduction   5
   The background to the comparative study   6

2 The patterns of crime   11
   The legal definition of rape   11
   The incidence and prevalence of rape   13

3 The investigative context   17
   Constitutional and procedural differences
   between the United States and the United
   Kingdom   17
   Rape as a political issue in the United
   States   21
   The results of research: the myths of rape   23
      The circumstances of the assault 24
      The reasons for sexual assault   26
   The results of research: rape trauma syndrome   28
   Rape crisis centres in the United States and
   the United Kingdom   31
   Medical services for victims   36

4 American police departments: four case studies   40
   Newark   40
   New York   41
   San Francisco   43
   Los Angeles   45
   Summary   46

5 The problems of sexual offence investigation   48
   Investigative problems common to crimes
   against the person   48

    Forensic evidence
    Identification of the unknown assailant
    Investigative problems specifically associated
    with sexual offences   51
        Non-reporting of offences
        False reporting and the withdrawal of
        complaints   53
        The defence of consent   62

6 The American approach to investigation   65
    Attitudinal change   65
    Interview techniques   66
    Training   69
    Liaison with non-police agencies   71
    Publicity   71

**7 Recommendations: Police in the United Kingdom—
towards a new approach**   73
    Medical procedures   74
    Specialist units or specially trained officers?   75
    Personnel   78
    Police interview procedure   79
    Training   81
        Recruit training   81
        Initial detective training   82
        Advanced detective training   82
        Higher police training   83
    Police policy on liaison and publicity   83
        Liaison with non-police bodies   83
        Publicity   85

8 Conclusion   87

Appendix A: Extract from *Survivor*. Booklet prepared by
Los Angeles Commission on Assaults Against Women

Appendix B: Cities having rape crisis centres in the United
Kingdom, November 1983   92

Appendix C: Information leaflet for victims
treated by Sexual Trauma Services, San Francisco   93

Appendix D: Information leaflet for victims.
Association of Police Surgeons of Great Britain   94

Appendix E: Rape trauma syndrome. A guide. Sexual
Trauma Services, San Francisco   95

Appendix F: *Beware. . .be aware.* New York Police
Department   99

Appendix G: *Silence frees a rapist to strike again!* Newark
Police Department   101

References   103

Index   106

TABLES AND FIGURES

Tables

2.1	The incidence of rape in the United States	13
2.2	The incidence of rape in England and Wales	14
3.1	Comparative statistics of the relationship of offender to victim and the location of the offence	24
3.2	Violence associated with rape. Philadelphia, 1958 and 1960	25
3.3	View taken of rape crisis centres by police in the United States	33
3.4	View taken of rape crisis centres by provincial police forces in the United Kingdom	34
4.1	Sexual offences investigated by the SARA Unit, Newark Police Department, 1975-1981	40
4.2	Cases of sexual assault investigated by the Sex Crimes Detail, San Francisco Police Department, 1980-1982	43
5.1	Methods used by United States police departments to identify unknown assailants and the success of those methods	49
5.2	Comparison of actual and reported crime rates in the United States	52
5.3	Final disposition of rape allegations in the United States, 1977	56
5.4	Detection rates for six United States police departments	60
7.1	Time of day and days of the week when rapes are reported, United States and Scotland	76

Figures

2.1	The incidence of rape in the United States, England and Wales and the Metropolitan Police District: cumulative year on year percentage increase, 1972-1982	15

FOREWORD

Investigating rape: A new approach for police is an important study and I am pleased to have an opportunity to contribute to it. Rape is more than a sexual crime; it is an act of violence against women which causes the victims to feel degradation, humiliation and shame.

In his book, Detective Inspector Blair puts forward a number of fundamental recommendations for improvements in the police investigation of sexual offences and these are now under consideration by a Metropolitan Police working party. Indeed, it has already been accepted by the working party that the investigation of rape and related sexual offences requires a highly selective degree of training for all officers throughout the Force.

The Police Foundation, of which I am a trustee, seeks to achieve a significant increase in the sum of useful knowledge available about policing problems, methods and organisation, and the wider dissemination of relevant practical information about policing and police community relations. The first study produced by the Police Foundation, *Road users and the police,* fulfilled these objectives but, like much other published work on the police service, it was prepared by independent researchers. Ian Blair's book is a good example of research carried out by a serving police officer and readers should find it most useful.

It would be quite wrong for research into any discipline to be conducted only by practitioners of that discipline, but I see this study as a sign of the determination of the police service to examine its procedures and practices objectively and to be able to respond effectively to social changes.

In recent years, sexual assault and its investigation have been the subject of heightened public concern and critics of police conduct in this area have been vociferous. It is now timely for a police voice to be heard in the debate in the form of thoroughly prepared and well-presented research. In offering this, the police contribute to the maintenance and development of good working relationships between the service and the public by bringing to their attention some of the problems police have to face. It is with this in mind that the author recommends harnessing the co-operation of the community in trying to prevent such crimes and, with the help of victim support schemes, to minimise the effects of rape upon the victim. I agree with this approach because it serves to emphasise the vitality of the links between the service and the community it serves.

Detective Inspector Blair's book ends with the words:

> . . . it is police officers to whom many rape victims turn at the moment of their greatest distress. This is a grave responsibility. I believe that it can most properly be discharged by the creation and maintenance of a whole approach, 'a new approach', to the investigation of rape.

I may say that I support this belief.

Sir Kenneth Newman

ACKNOWLEDGEMENTS

During the period of my research for this study, I have received assistance and friendship on both sides of the Atlantic from many police officers, medical personnel, lawyers and academics. Almost everyone with whom I have come into contact has displayed endless patience in providing me with information. I cannot acknowledge all of them, but I wish to record my special gratitude to those who were responsible for direct liaison with me during my visit to the United States: Lieutenant Kenneth Wilson, Newark Police Department, Inspector Garry Lemos, San Francisco Police Department and Detective Mae Taylor Johnson, Los Angeles Police Department. My particular thanks are also due to Linda Eberth, of the Sexual Trauma Service, San Francisco, Gail Abarbanel, of the Rape Treatment Center, Santa Monica and Harry O'Reilly, John Jay College, New York.

The extract from the booklet *Survivor* and the information leaflets for victims and about rape trauma syndrome at Appendices A, C, D and E appear by kind permission of the Los Angeles Commission on Assaults against Women, of the Sexual Trauma Service, San Francisco and the Association of Police Surgeons of Great Britain.

I also acknowledge with gratitude the generosity of the trustees of the Police Bursaries Trust in providing me with the opportunity to travel to the United States of America; the assistance of the Commissioner of Police of the Metropolis for the provision of additional funds and leave of absence to undertake the bursary; and the support of Mollie Weatheritt and Barrie Irving of the Police Foundation, who, together with Thelma Wagstaff of the Metropolitan Police, have given me encouragement in the completion of this study.

Ian Blair

For FJB

PREFACE

The chapters which follow review previous research on the effects of rape on victims and the investigation of rape, describe investigative practice in four United States city police departments and compare and contrast the American situation with police practice in the United Kingdom. From this analysis, I draw certain conclusions and make specific recommendations for the reform of relevant police practice in the United Kingdom.

The reader needs to keep a number of things in mind. First, the opinions expressed in these pages are mine alone and represent the official policy or views neither of the Metropolitan Police nor of the Home Office. I would, however, hope that there are some points at which my views would correspond with official opinion, and I am aware that, as a result of the findings of the research conducted for this study, a working party has been set up by the Metropolitan Police to consider its procedures in relation to the investigation of rape and kindred sexual offences. At the time of writing, this working party has recommended that certain changes in procedure and training, similar to those recommended in this study, should be implemented within the Metropolitan Police.

Secondly, the basic technique used by United States police officers is to deal with the victim on the grounds of an enhanced knowledge of the effects of rape upon the victim, and of the effects on that victim of the interaction between her and the investigator. In making a comparison between the United States and the United Kingdom, I have called these American techniques a 'new approach'. This may invite the criticism that some of the ideas incorporated within this approach are already well known.

This is, of course, true. The methods which I observed in the United States, however, are distinguished from British best practice by three characteristics: reliance on modern research, formal definition and homogeneity of procedure. The result is a restatement of traditional procedures, distinct from present British practice, and forming a whole greater, and newer, than the sum of its parts.

Thirdly, the emphasis of this study concerns the interface between the victim of rape and the police investigator. The investigation of a crime, however, depends for its success upon many other factors outside that relationship and, in particular, requires expertise and diligence in the interaction between the investigator and the alleged assailant. The fact that this study focuses upon police activity in relation to the victim reflects limitations of space and time, and does not imply that the skills involved in the apprehension and interviewing of the suspect are not of vital importance.

Fourthly, I must emphasis that I am aware that, despite regional variations in procedure, rape is regarded throughout the United Kingdom as a very serious crime, and is investigated with conscientious professional skill. This study should not be construed as implying any criticism of the diligence or detective ability of my colleagues. Nor should it be taken as vindicating general accusations of police inefficiency and callousness which have occasionally been made in recent years. Whilst there have obviously been episodes of crassness and inefficiency in the police treatment of rape victims, there will have been other cases characterised by excellent professional investigation. This research is not concerned with the relative size of these two categories.

Lastly, any study of the procedures to be followed in the treatment of victims can become overconcerned with the examination of administrative technicalities, thereby missing the point that the client, not its own procedures, is the reason for the existence of a caring agency. Much of this study is necessarily concerned with police and related procedures; it is, however, written in the hope that it may contribute to a lessening of the suffering which is the invariable experience of every victim of sexual assault.

Rape is not primarily a sexual act. . .
Rape is primarily an act of violence with sex as the weapon.

Ann Burgess and Lynda Holmstrom, 'Rape trauma syndrome',
American Journal of Psychiatry, September 1974

1 INTRODUCTION

This study owes its origin to exploratory research on the investigation of rape carried out by the author at the Police Staff College at Bramshill in 1978. That research examined the literature concerning the effects of rape upon its victims and included a limited survey of responses to the crime by police in England and Wales. Very simply stated, its conclusions were that the effects of rape upon its victims appeared to be more severe than in the case of almost any other crime, and that neither the police, the criminal justice system nor the main caring agencies were taking sufficient account of the severity of this impact either to minimise the traumatic effect of the crime on the victim or to maximise the chance of convicting the assailant.

While the results of this research were both surprising and intriguing, they would have been unlikely to prompt further work but for the impact of the experiences of the author when subsequently working in a busy criminal investigation department in an inner-city area of London. Here, while investigating a number of offences of rape, he became acutely and personally aware of the impact of rape on its victims and their families. This led directly to a decision to continue the research work begun at Bramshill.

During the next three years, the conclusions of the Bramshill study were evaluated against data and personal experience in relation to cases investigated by the author and his colleagues from the time of first report to the final court of trial. From observation of those victims and their cases, it was apparent that the conclusions of the earlier study were broadly correct, and it began to seem feasible that knowledge of the effects of rape upon victims might ultimately improve both their treatment, and, possibly, the likelihood of the detection and conviction of the offender.

The bibliographic review undertaken as part of the Bramshill study had shown the extent of academic research work on rape in the United States. There were also reports of far-reaching changes in investigative methods implemented by a number of American police departments. These innovations created the possibility of a comparative study of police methods used in the investigation of rape

6 Introduction

and kindred sexual offences in the United Kingdom and the United States.

With the assistance of a grant from the Police Bursaries Trust, the author conducted further research in the United States in September 1982. Four American police departments were selected as field sites: Newark, New York, San Francisco and Los Angeles. Background information about these police departments is given in Chapter 4.

The findings of this study were first published in an official report to the Home Office (Blair, 1982). This has now been revised and updated to include the results of a further limited survey of police procedures in England and Wales. The present edition also takes into account the 1983 Home Office Circular on the Investigation of Offences of Rape; the report by Chambers and Millar from the Central Research Unit of the Scottish Office entitled *Investigating sexual assault* (1983); and the *Fifteenth report* (on sexual offences) of the Criminal Law Revision Committee (1984).

The background to the comparative study

The incidence of rape in England and Wales is steadily increasing (see Table 2.2). As it increases, the importance of police procedures in relation to sexual assault and the importance of the overall police approach to sexual assault victims will also increase. The *British crime survey* (Hough and Mayhew, 1983) also noted an incidence of fear of sexual assault substantially greater than the occurrence of the crime.

There appears to be room for a reappraisal of current police procedure and this study is designed to consider ways in which such procedure could be examined and improved. The study is based upon the assumption that the best approach to that reappraisal is through an examination of the experience of police departments in the United States of America. This assumption is itself based upon the scale of recent American research into rape and its investigation, and the comparability of social development between the United Kingdom and the United States. In the early 1970s, American police procedures in relation to the investigation of rape underwent fundamental development, as a result of a marked increase in the incidence of rape coinciding with important changes in American politics and society. In 1974, the crime of forcible rape had not only increased more than other crimes against the person (by 116 per cent over the previous decade), it also had the lowest arrest rate (51 per cent) (Federal Bureau of Investigation). This occurred at the very period during which the American women's movement underwent its main expansion in both energy and influence. In the early 1970s, therefore, many American police departments and the United States Department of Justice found themselves faced with an intense challenge as to the effectiveness of policing methods and structures designed to deal with the crime of rape (see Brownmiller, 1975; Russell, 1975; *Forcible rape*, Vol. 1, 1977). Under this pressure, many American police departments began examining their approach to rape investigation and, in particular, their relationship with those organisations which criticised them from positions both inside and on the fringes of the criminal justice system (see, for example, Queen's Bench Foundation, 1975).

In an attempt to forestall both the rising incidence of rape and the rising chorus of criticism as to their failure to deal adequately with it, law enforcement agencies in the United States have expended very considerable amounts of energy and finance in an examination of rape investigation. Different methods of manpower allocation, training, administrative structure, accountability to and involvement of the public and forensic examination have been considered and evaluated. The result has been a fundamental change in the approach of investigators to the victim, and a consequent increase in the perceived quality of service to victims and the public at large. Experimentation in the United States has shown that while very little can be done to increase the detection rate in cases involving attacks by unknown assailants, the methods employed by American rape investigators decrease the trauma suffered by victims and appear to improve the quality of evidence and crime intelligence they can provide.

In past decades, many social developments in the United States (from an increase in drug abuse and racially-fuelled disorder to an increased concern with consumer and minority rights) have proved to be an accelerated and exaggerated version of subsequent developments in the United Kingdom. The thesis behind this book is that an increase in the occurrence of rape may be a similar social and criminological issue, and that the sheer scale of American research and innovation in this field cannot be ignored and should be examined. The case for a comparative study, therefore, rests upon the opportunity which the American situation affords for the evaluation of developments in police procedures in an environment in many ways similar to that of the United Kingdom.

The value of insights derived from this kind of cross-cultural comparison, however, depends to a considerable degree on the ability to discern the effect of cultural differences. Many of the characteristics of rape and its investigation appear to be shared by Western, industrialised societies with police forces operating within a common law tradition. Many of the innovations in the United States should, therefore, be relevant to the United Kingdom. Some of the new American methods, however, have not been successful; some involve the allocation of resources and manpower on a scale which could not be warranted by the present incidence of rape in the United Kingdom. Some of the techniques depend on the American culture for their effectiveness and could not easily be transferred to British practice. Many of the best results, however, have been obtained as a result of simple changes in procedure and limited additions to training which are unaffected by these reservations. It is hoped, therefore, that this study may be of practical use in the reappraisal of British police procedure relating to the investigation of sexual assault.

A decade has passed since demands for police reform resulted in far-reaching changes in rape investigation in the United States. This study is also designed to evaluate those changes ten years after their introduction and from the perspective of a different culture, and to comment on the impact of changes in American political priorities in relation to crime. There would be little force behind these aims, however, if public disquiet about rape was negligible in either the United Kingdom or the United States. A brief review of a few recent cases serves to indicate that the current level of public concern is still substantial.

In the United States, intense public controversy was aroused at the beginning of 1984 by the Big Dan's Tavern case in which an entire rape trial from Fall River, Massachusetts was televised nationwide, resulting in the destruction of the anonymity of the victim. This had severe consequences for other rape trials. Once again, police, medical and judicial procedures in relation to rape, together with American media ethics, are under particular scrutiny.

There is mounting evidence that the pressure for reform experienced by American police departments is also occurring in the United Kingdom. In early 1982, public controversy was aroused by judicial comment about a rape victim displaying 'contributory negligence' by hitch-hiking.[1] Later in the year there was grave disquiet over a decision to offer no evidence in a celebrated case of rape in Scotland,[2] disquiet so widespread that it led to the resignation of a government minister, the Solicitor General for Scotland. Soon afterwards, a police interview of an alleged rape victim was broadcast on television during which the investigating officers seemed to display inept and unprofessional conduct.[3] 1983 ended with the publication of Chambers' and Millar's report, *Investigating sexual assault*, which suggested fundamental shortcomings in police procedures and attitudes in Scotland.[4] There have been similar periods in the past in which events—usually particular court cases—have served to arouse public concern; most notably *DPP v Morgan*[5] which resulted in a change of legislation and what is known as 'The Guardsman case', *(R v Holdsworth)*.[6] However, few police initiatives have resulted from these surges of public and judicial interest and even the most noteworthy one, the creation of specialist rape units in Thames Valley, has been limited to assigning non-detective officers to make preliminary contact with the victim.

In contrast to the United States, the British social research community has also been relatively inactive on the subject of rape. Most research and comment in Britain has dealt only tangentially with the effects of rape on the victim and with methods of investigation. Few studies have attempted an in-depth cross-cultural comparison. Shapland (1981) and Adler (1982) have examined the interrelation of the victim and the courts. Walmsley and White (1979) have examined sentencing patterns. Smart (1976) and also Edwards (1981) have examined the wider relationship between gender and crime. The exceptions have been the reports of the Rape Counselling and Research Projects (London Rape Crisis Centre, 1978a, 1982) and Chambers and Millar, neither of which, however, draws together the findings of American and British research or examines them in the context both of present police procedures and the constraints on reform. It is hoped that this study may to some degree repair that omission, and prepare the ground for further and more academically rigorous investigation.

Notes

1. Not reported. Trial at Ipswich Crown Court, February 1982.
2. Bill for Criminal Letters: CH. Justiciary Office Edinburgh, 1 April 1982.

10 *Introduction*

3. The film of the Thames Valley interview was broadcast on 18 January 1982, and was widely reported on 19 and 20 January 1982.

4. The study by Chambers and Millar was published shortly before this report went to press and the thesis advanced here draws extensively on its findings. While its conclusions are comprehensively documented, a note of caution should be sounded about at least one of its seminal sources, an article by Detective Sergeant Firth of the West Midlands Police. The author has not yet met a police officer whose reaction to this article, which appears to recommend police to display harshness towards rape victims, has not been one of complete disagreement. The article, which was originally published in *Police Review* in 1975, is reprinted in full on pp. 83-4 of *Investigatimg sexual assault*.

5. (1975) Cr. App. Rep. 136.

6. Not reported. Trial at Central Criminal Court, 1978.

2 THE PATTERNS OF CRIME

The legal definition of rape

Following the case of *DPP v Morgan*, and the subsequent report of the Advisory Group on the Law of Rape (Home Office, 1975), a new legal definition of rape was enacted in England and Wales. Section 1 (1) of The Sexual Offences (Amendment) Act 1976 provides that:

A man commits rape if
a) he has unlawful sexual intercourse with a woman who at the time of the intercourse does not consent to it, and
b) at that time, he knows she does not consent to the intercourse or is reckless as to whether she consents to it.

The maximum punishment for rape is imprisonment for life. Sexual intercourse with females under 16 years of age and under 13 years of age is termed unlawful sexual intercourse, and is prohibited by Sections 5 and 6, Sexual Offences Act 1956, which provide different punishments for offences on girls of these different ages. Legally, rape or unlawful sexual intercourse must be by intromission of the penis into the vagina. With the exception of intromission of the penis into the anus, termed buggery, and prohibited under Section 12, Sexual Offences Act 1956, almost all other forms of sexual assault are dealt with under the provisions of Sections 14 and 15, Sexual Offences Act 1956 and are termed indecent assaults. These different sections and other enactments provide different penalties for indecent assaults on the two sexes and on children of different ages. The fifteenth report of the Criminal Law Revision Committee, on sexual offences, has recommended no substantial changes in the Sexual Offences Acts in regard either to the definition of rape or the delineation of other relevant types of sexual assault. It has, however, recommended that the maximum penalty for attempted rape should be raised from seven years imprisonment to imprisonment for life and that the maximum penalty for an indecent assault on a female should be raised from two years to ten years imprisonment, the present maximum penalty for such an offence against a male.

Rape and kindred sexual assaults are offences against the penal codes of the different states of the United States, and are not offences under federal law, except under wholly exceptional circumstances. Each state is responsible for the wording of its penal code and no single definition of any sexual offence can be given for the whole of the United States. However, United States law is generally based upon the law of England and Wales, and follows broadly similar lines. In general terms, the English crime of rape is known in the United States as forcible rape, and that of unlawful sexual intercourse as statutory rape. The crime of buggery is normally termed sodomy, but indecent assaults are subdivided into a great number of divergent statutes. Different states have offences of oral copulation, oral sodomy, criminal sexual contact, aggravated sexual assault, child molestation or indecent assault on minors. In a very few jurisdictions, for example in the State of Michigan, no distinction is drawn between forcible rape by the penis into the vagina and the insertion of other items into the vagina, or of the penis into other orifices. A suggestion that these distinctions should also be abolished in the United Kingdom has been rejected by the Criminal Law Revision Committee.

In order to make this report more comprehensible, English terms will be used throughout. The American offence of forcible rape will be termed rape, and that of statutory rape, unlawful sexual intercourse; sodomy will be referred to as buggery, and the term indecent assault will be used to cover all other forms of assault in circumstances of indecency.

Forced sexual intercourse within marriage is excluded from the English definition of rape, although other sexual offences can be committed by one spouse upon the other. A number of jurisdictions in the United States, including California, have now provided that rape by a husband on his wife is an offence, and this is termed 'spousal rape'. The Criminal Law Revision Committee's fifteenth report rejected the general widening of English rape legislation to include offences by husbands upon their wives, but has recommended that the offence should be capable of commission by a husband actually, in addition to judicially (the present state of case law), separated from his wife.

Scottish law appears already to accept the possibility of rape by a husband on his wife (Criminal Law Revision Committee, 1984, pp.

18-19); South Australia, Victoria and New South Wales have altered their criminal codes to include the possibility of spousal rape. As in the United States, prosecutions appear to have been rare in these jurisdictions, and future legal reform in this direction in England and Wales appears unlikely to affect police methods, other than by increasing the ever-present need for particular sensitivity on behalf of the investigator.

Homosexual offences are not dealt with in this study; nevertheless in some homosexual cases, as in certain other types of heterosexual offences such as incest, the methods of investigation outlined and recommended in this study may be appropriate.

The incidence and prevalence of rape

Rape has been called 'the all-American crime' (Griffin, 1975). In the United States, the incidence of rape has increased sharply over the last two decades, although the national total of offences for 1981 and 1982 shows a decrease in comparison to 1980. American commentators suggest that this decrease is due to deterrent sentencing policies introduced in many states, and probably more significantly, to the fact that the American population profile is ageing and that rape is a crime committed primarily by young men.[1] Nevertheless, the incidence of rape in 1982 represents an 83.8 per cent increase over the figure for 1972. Table 2.1 gives details of all forcible rapes known to police in the United States.

Table 2.1: The incidence of rape in the United States

Year	Number recorded	Rate per 100,000 females
1970	37,860	35
1971	42,120	39
1972	46,690	43
1973	51,230	47
1974	55,210	51
1975	56,090	52
1976	56,730	52
1977	63,020	58
1978	67,131	61
1979	75,989	69
1980	82,088	75
1981	81,536	74
1982	77,763	71

Source: Federal Bureau of Investigation.

14 *The patterns of crime*

Official statistics appear to suggest that the occurrence of rape in the United Kingdom is far less frequent than in the United States. Table 2.2 gives details of offences of rape known to police forces in England and Wales and the Metropolitan Police in particular.

Table 2.2: The incidence of rape in England and Wales

Year	Metropolitan Police	England and Wales	Rate per 100,000 females, England and Wales
1972	135	893	3.7
1973	132	998	4.1
1974	156	1,052	4.4
1975	167	1,040	4.3
1976	181	1,094	4.6
1977	187	1,015	4.2
1978	275	1,243	5.2
1979	246	1,170	4.9
1980	266	1,225	5.1
1981	256	1,068	4.4
1982	285	1,336	5.5
1983	317	1,334	5.5

Source: *Criminal statistics England and Wales* and *Reports of the Commissioner of Police of the Metropolis.*

The statistics in Tables 2.1 and 2.2 indicate that rape is between ten and fifteen times more prevalent in the United States than in the United Kingdom. The incidence of recorded rape in each of the cities visited in this study, for instance, was at least 20 times that recorded for London. However, the statistics for England and Wales and the Metropolitan Police may conceal two significant points: the accuracy of the recorded figures and the rate of increase in the incidence of rape. As far as the first point is concerned, Chapter 5 examines the low reporting rate for rape in comparison to that for other crimes. It is quite clear that reported rape does not accurately represent actual incidence in either the United States or the United Kingdom. While it is true that rape in the United States occurs far more frequently than in the United Kingdom and 'repeater' or recidivist offenders are also more common in America, it may still be the case that police and public policies in the United States are more effective in encouraging victims to report offences. If this argument is correct, then the official figures for the occurrence of rape in the United Kingdom would represent a smaller proportion of the actual level of crime than do the official statistics in the United States.

Secondly, the sheer size of the disparity in actual numbers of recorded offences between the United States and the United Kingdom conceals the fact that the rate of increase of offences is similar. Figure 2.1 presents changes in the patterns of incidence of rape in the two countries as cumulative frequency curves for the years 1972 to 1982.

Figure 2.1: The incidence of rape in the United States, England and Wales and the Metropolitan Police District: cumulative year on year percentage increase, 1972–1982

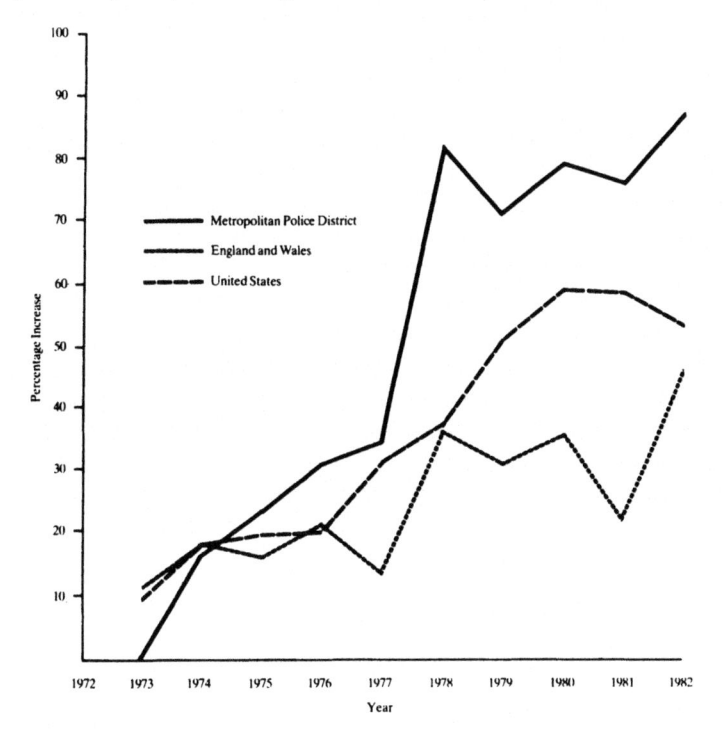

Figure 2.1 shows that although rape per 100,000 females is far more frequent in the United States, the rate of increase in the occurrence of this offence for the Metropolitan Police District between 1973 and 1982 was greater than the rate of increase for the United States as a whole. The corresponding pattern of increase for England and Wales is less dramatic and is, of course, markedly affected by what has happened in London. The graph may be taken as a further indication of the validity of comparing the two countries

particularly where urban areas of the United Kingdom are involved. This cross-cultural similarity, however, does not extend to rates of detection. At first sight, a comparison of the American clearance rate of 51 per cent in 1982 does not compare favourably with a clear-up rate of 70 per cent in England and Wales or 55 per cent in the Metropolitan Police District. However, the format of United States crime statistics is different from that in the United Kingdom. In particular, the concepts of offences cleared (United States) and crimes cleared up (United Kingdom) are not wholly comparable. As indicated in Chapter 5, there is some evidence that the relatively high clear-up rate in England and Wales is a reflection of police recording practices peculiar to rape.

For this reason, this study can only suggest, rather than prove, that the 'new approach' adopted by American police departments improves the possibility of detection. This issue will be discussed in greater detail in Chapter 5, but some light can be thrown on it by comparing American police performance in relation to rape with their performance in relation to other crimes.

In this context it is of interest to note that while the incidence of rape rose by 41 per cent in the United States between 1974 and 1982, the clearance rate remained the same at 51 per cent. During the same period the incidence of homicide increased by 2 per cent, while the clear-up rate declined by 6 per cent. Similarly, aggravated assaults (equivalent to grievous bodily harm in England and Wales) increased by 16 per cent, while the clear-up rate declined by 38 per cent. These figures may, of course, reflect the increase in the resources applied to rape investigation as well as improvements in methods of investigation.

Note

1. Forty-seven per cent of offenders are believed to be under 25 (*Forcible rape*, 1977. Vol. XI. p. 69). Fifty-two per cent of arrests are under 25 (*Uniform crime reports*, Federal Bureau of Investigation, 1982, p. 15).

3 THE INVESTIGATIVE CONTEXT

Examining the methods used by police in the United States in the investigation of rape and comparing them with police practice in the United Kingdom can only be useful to readers on either side of the Atlantic if set in the context of relevant legal, political and social differences between the two countries. This chapter therefore deals first with the differences between the American and British police and judicial systems and considers the pressure in the United States in recent years to reform rape investigation. Subsequent sections of the chapter are concerned with the results of that pressure; the increase in knowledge concerning the nature of the crime and its effects; and developments in the pattern of medico-social assistance available to the victims of rape in the United States.

Constitutional and procedural differences between the United States and the United Kingdom

Any comparison of policing between two countries must take account of dissimilarities in the constitutions and legal systems within which police operate. This is particularly true in the case of comparison between the United States and the United Kingdom, because similarities of language and of the common law tradition can obscure very important differences.

The most immediately significant difference between the two countries lies in the diversity of law enforcement agencies in the United States. Like the United Kingdom, the United States does not have a national police force. In the field of law enforcement, the only federal agency is the Federal Bureau of Investigation, which is concerned only with federal crimes (that is crimes against federal law, or crimes in the perpetration of which offenders cross state boundaries or use interstate facilities). All other agencies are locally based and locally controlled. However, while the 43 police forces in England and Wales all have establishments of more than 900 officers, with standards of recruitment, equipment and inspection co-ordinated by central government, the United States has a multiplicity of law enforcement agencies with very little central coordination or control. In the county of Greater Los Angeles, for example, there are some 50 law enforcement agencies, which range in size from the 7,000 officers of the Los Angeles Police Department to departments of only two or three men. The effect of this multiplicity of agencies, with different sizes and capabilities, is that policies and effectiveness are far from uniform. Thus, some of the recent innovations in methods of rape investigation implemented by the most forward-looking agencies have not been adopted by neighbouring units.

The existence of prosecuting authorities separate from the police represents another major difference. Criminal cases in the United States are not prosecuted, as they normally are in England and Wales, by or on behalf of the police, but by an independent district attorney, whose role is similar to that of the procurator fiscal in Scotland. Unlike the procurator fiscal, however, the district attorney has his own investigators who continue or conclude the police investigation. The theoretical advantages of this system are that it should provide a uniformity of prosecutorial approach and can involve the attorney who will ultimately present the case at an early stage in the investigation; it provides the detective with a point of referral on matters of law and practice; and it lifts from the detective the burden of the decision to continue or not to continue with proceedings. The disadvantages are that the detective does not have the final responsibility for the completion of the case and it is, therefore, usual for detectives to complete their investigation at an earlier stage and therefore in not as much detail as is normal practice in the United Kingdom. Even more important, the reputation of district attorneys and their deputies is often founded on a record of successful prosecution; during the fieldwork for this study, the author was aware of a strong feeling among police that, even where some credible evidence exists against a suspect, district attorneys are unlikely to proceed with cases in which the outcome of a trial is uncertain. It is interesting that institutionalised friction between detectives and district attorneys is a traditional feature of American crime fiction.

The only independent prosecuting authority in England and Wales is the office of the Director of Public Prosecutions, which considers only offences of particular gravity and, in the case of rape, only certain kinds of multiple offences. However, the Director of Public Prosecutions operates a standard rule across the whole of England and Wales by which prosecutions are not normally pursued in cases considered to have less than a 50 per cent chance of success. No such formal rule operates among district attorneys and it is likely that criteria for prosecution vary from one area of the United States to another.

The independent prosecutorial system currently being considered for England and Wales is likely to be closer to the procurator fiscal than the district attorney system and its introduction will only partially reconcile the differences between the two countries.

Uniformed patrol officers in the United States perform work which has traditionally been regarded as the responsibility of detectives in the United Kingdom; together with the existence of district attorneys, this allocation of work to patrol officers narrows the function of detectives in the United States. This is reflected in the hours worked by detectives. *Rape and its victims*, a survey conducted in 1974 by the Center for Women Policy Studies, found that the majority of sexual offence investigation units surveyed operated an 8-hour office day, although there were call-out procedures. The fieldwork for this study indicated that few detectives in this kind of unit expected to work unsocial hours or overtime. This reflects general practice among detectives in the United States. Los Angeles, for instance, normally has only a single team of detectives working in the evening, and a single team working at night to deal with every scene of major crime across the whole city.

This allocation of work has the effect of passing the burden of initial investigation, both of the scene and of the victim, from the detective to the patrol officer. The seizure of forensic evidence and the overseeing of evidence collection by medical staff are routinely carried out by officers other than detectives. It is by no means universal procedure for detectives to visit crime scenes. In the United States, this has meant that some of the responsibility for the treatment of rape victims by police falls to patrol officers, whereas in Britain it is the detective who is most involved with the victim.

It is also important to note that in United States police departments the detective force, called the detective bureau, is traditionally divided into specialist squads. Many police departments maintain only a central detective bureau, but even where, as in Los Angeles or New York, bureaux are stationed at local police stations, each detective will be responsible for only one sort of crime. The development of specialist rape squads in the United States is a natural consequence of this model of detective deployment.

The last major difference in terms of police organisation concerns the position and method of selection of American chief officers of police. Although very senior police officers in the United Kingdom are, except in London, selected by a process which involves some degree of local democratic influence, many senior police posts in the United States are direct political appointments. In some cases, these posts are open to individuals with no previous police experience — in this study, Newark provided an example of this type of appointment. This method of selection, and its corollary, the method of dismissal, renders police departments in the United States far more sensitive to political and social change than is the case in the United Kingdom.

Differences in the laws concerning the admissibility of evidence will also affect the police handling of cases of sexual assault. The *Miranda Rules*[1] governing the interrogation of suspects provide more detailed safeguards for the accused in the United States and, in theory, correspondingly greater restrictions for the investigator, than do the *Judges' Rules* in the United Kingdom (Home Office, 1978). On the other hand, rules governing identification by identification parades, known as line-ups, are much less stringent in the United States.

Three major issues divide the two jurisdictions at trial. First the system of plea bargaining, not yet fully acknowledged in the United Kingdom, is a major feature of the United States judicial administration, and is frequently used in sexual offence cases. Secondly, in the United States the principle and practice of jury vetting is fully accepted. During the *voir dire* in the United States, both prosecution and defence counsel question potential jurors as to their attitudes to the crime, to the ethnic background of the accused and of the victim, and about their own marital status, education, background and religious convictions. This questioning enables respective counsel to remove potential jurors with unacceptable views, or an apparent degree of intelligence which it is thought might prejudice them unduly in favour of the prosecution or defence. After this, however, only unanimous verdicts are acceptable. Lastly, in California, where much of this study was conducted, the defendant retains the common law right to remain silent in court. If, however, he decides to give evidence and enters the witness box, his previous convictions are communicated to the jury.

All these factors must be borne in mind when comparisons are made between the United Kingdom and the United States. Their effect is to render the contrast of statistics less of a comparison of exact levels of crime and more of an indication of trends within each country. Equally important, these judicial and police practices must be understood as part of the background to the developments which have affected rape investigation in the last two decades, and which will now be examined.

Rape as a political issue in the United States

The late 1960s and early 1970s, the years in which rape increased most dramatically, were also the years during which the women's movement in the United States first came to prominence. Rape is a crime committed only against women and only by men, and it can be said to involve the degradation and exploitation of female sexuality by men. In the 1960s, in America as everywhere, this crime against women was investigated almost exclusively by men, and there was some truth in the allegation that it was being investigated ineffectively. The women's movement seized upon rape as a symbol: it was possible to interpret the crime as a feature of the suppression of the rights of women by men in a patriarchal society. The women's movement declared that the prevention and detection of rape was a matter for women, and an issue which would unite and mobilise many women behind the movement. In this, Brownmiller's *Against our will* proved to be a clarion call.

It was a particularly potent argument. Furthermore, the issue was a convenient one for politicians to encourage in order to indicate a concern for women's rights. Between 1973 and 1981 the United States government disbursed grants for the study of rape and sexual assault to an estimated value of $125 million.[2] While most of the research funds were directed through the Law Enforcement Assistance Administration—part of the United States Department of Justice—the government also established the National Center for the Prevention and Control of Rape within the Department of Health, Education and Welfare. Grants were awarded to city and county authorities to establish programmes of rape prevention and preventive education, and to institute or to reform special sexual assault investigation units. A great number of grants was awarded to individual researchers and to interested groups for research into particular aspects of the crime and its effects. Particularly important fields of study were criminal justice administration, medical and

22 The investigative context

psychological care of victims, community education and involvement, rape prevention and the interaction and interdependence of these various subject areas.

The Law Enforcement Assistance Administration itself conducted a three-year nationwide survey of the incidence of rape, the characteristics of the offender and his victim, and the methods, training and administrative structures used in the investigation of the crime. This important research—from 1975 to 1978—resulted in the eleven-volume federal report *Forcible rape* but the variety, utility and complexity of other research should not be underrated. For instance, the bibliography and the list of grants awarded by the National Center for the Prevention and Control of Rape run to over 50 pages.

However, because of the political pressure for reform and the enthusiasm of the women's movement, this volume of research produced certain recommendations for change which were subsequently found to be ineffective, or insupportable in terms of expense. Among the former was the institution of all-female rape squads, and among the latter the inauguration of over-complex rape analysis units, particularly in the larger conurbations, as is described below in relation to Los Angeles and New York.

Nevertheless, the effects of the political and public interest in rape investigation were largely beneficial. The nationwide research discovered some obviously remediable faults in the United States system of justice. Some states had required a degree of corroboration of force, of sexual penetration and of lack of consent such as to preclude almost any successful prosecution. These state laws were reformed and, in many states, legislation was enacted to protect the anonymity of victims[3] and to prevent the examination of evidence concerning the past sexual history of the victim. American legislation on these points now closely resembles the Sexual Offences (Amendment) Act 1976. However, after these obvious goals had been achieved, and state laws from California to New York had been revised, critical attention began to focus on two specific areas of concern: the effect of rape upon the victim, and the methods used by investigators in the successful apprehension of the suspect. It is these two issues which are dealt with at length in this study.

The results of research: the myths of rape

Of all crimes, rape and murder most intrigue the public at large. Popular fiction and the press frequently contain lurid details of both crimes and, as a result, both rape and murder are surrounded by a body of received public wisdom considerably at variance with reality. In both cases, the crime, its perpetrators and their victims are obscured by myths, easily disprovable, but which form part of the common consciousness of both men and women.

Much of the literature on rape, and much of the explanatory material currently distributed for use by victims of sexual assault, deal with the mythology of rape. For instance, the booklet describing their activities issued by the London Rape Crisis Centre (1982) and the longer booklet, *Survivor*, given to all sexual assault victims by the Los Angeles Police Department (see extract at Appendix A), both contain references to the existence of certain myths about rape. They suggest that common beliefs about rape tend to cluster in the following four contradictory groups of attitudes:

> That the rape will have been committed by a stranger in a dark alley or similar location.
> That the victim will have fought back desperately, but will eventually enjoy the experience when her resistance is overcome (a particularly male attitude).
> That rape is physically impossible without the victim's consent, and that the victim is responsible for the attack in any event ('nice girls don't get raped').
> That rape arises from the sexual urges of normal men in some way frustrated, but that many rapists are actually maniacs.

Myths surrounding homicide are of little significance to the investigation of the crime, but American police have realised that it is possible for beliefs about rape to affect deeply the victim, her relationship with the investigator and the course of the investigation itself. United States sex crimes investigators are therefore made aware of the difference between commonly-held opinions concerning rape and the findings of research. These differences are also applicable to the United Kingdom, and are therefore considered here.

The four clusters of beliefs referred to above can be further classified into those which relate to the circumstances of the assault, and those which relate to the reasons behind it. The research findings reproduced here are principally derived from the United States but, where possible, additional material from the United Kingdom has been included.

The circumstances of the assault

a. Relationship of the offender and location of the offence. The suggestion that rape is principally a crime committed by strangers, or that it most commonly occurs out of doors is not borne out by research. Table 3.1 contrasts the findings of an early but important American study, Amir's *Patterns of forcible rape* (1971), based on an analysis of rapes recorded by police in Philadelphia in 1958 and 1960, with statistics reproduced by the London Rape Crisis Centre (1982) and the Birmingham Rape Crisis Centre (1981) in recent reports. These figures are also supported by the findings of *Forcible rape* (Vol. I, p. 20) and Chambers and Millar (p. 18).

Table 3.1: Comparative statistics of the relationship of offender to victim and the location of the offence

	Amir 1958–60 %	London Rape Crisis Centre 1978–9 %	Birmingham Rape Crisis Centre 1980 %
Relationship			
Stranger	42.3	46	52.3
Acquaintance	24.0	38	31.4
Friend	24.6	9	5.8
Lover	6.0	4	3.5
Relative	2.5	3	7.0
Location			
Indoors	51.6	60	51.3
Outdoors	48.4	40	48.7

The table indicates that about half of all rapists are strangers. This first statistic is an indication of a feature found in much of the rest of the mythology; the myth of the stranger rapist is not entirely untrue, but is the most frightening aspect of the crime, and it is this frightening aspect that is exaggerated to become the whole belief. Thus it becomes possible to consider that victims who have not been raped by strangers have not been raped at all.

b. Victim resistance. It is widely believed that women will resist rape at all costs, as a 'fate worse than death'. Amir found, however, that only 18 per cent of victims had fought back, while 27 per cent went as far as to scream and to try to escape. Fifty-five per cent described themselves as being totally submissive (Amir, p. 167).

c. Violence suffered and the concept of victim enjoyment. It is unlikely that the 55 per cent were submissive because they were really enjoying the experience, which is a pervasive male impression. Once again, it was Amir's findings which first cast serious doubt on this possibility. Table 3.2 shows the amount of violence suffered by victims in Amir's study.

Table 3.2: Violence associated with rape. Philadelphia, 1958 and 1960

No violence	Roughness	Non-brutal beating before rape	Non-brutal beating during and after rape	Beaten brutally before rape	Beaten brutally during and after rape	Choked
%	%	%	%	%	%	%
14.9	28.5	21.8	2.9	10.6	9.8	11.5

It would be very surprising if the rape was enjoyed by the 85.1 per cent of rape victims who endured physical violence, or the 31.9 per cent who received a choking or brutal physical abuse, and would bear its marks. Visible injuries would also have been discernible in 39.8 per cent of the victims whose cases were examined by Chambers and Millar (p. 20).

The idea of victim enjoyment is widely found in pornography. It is sustained by the existence of a variety of sexual attitudes, the description and explanation of which lie beyond the scope of this study. There is no rational basis for these attitudes which are explained very concisely by Ogden Nash:

> Seduction is for sissies
> A He-man wants his rape

Men seem to find it difficult to think of rape in non-sexual terms. Perhaps this is because sexual activity for them almost always contains an element of aggression symbolised by erection and penetration; and the exaggeration and distortion of this element in rape is still not sufficient to force men to define rape as mere violence. Women have no such difficulty.

The reasons for sexual assault

The second type of belief about sexual assault concerns the motives and prior behaviour of victim and assailant.

a. The impossibility of rape. There is a theory—colloquially expressed as 'you can't thread a moving needle'—that consent is necessary for sexual intercourse; in Americanese:

> because of the almost inexpugnable position she occupies on account of the topography of the sexual organs in the female body (Mendelson, quoted in Amir).

This theory completely ignores the disparity in physical strength between an assailant or assailants and the victim, the capacity of a surprise attack to neutralise resistance, and a fear of bodily harm greater than fear of sexual violation. June and Joseph Csida, in their book on the avoidance of rape, quote a passage from Thompson's *Hell's Angels*, which summarises the rejection of this belief:

> Any lawyer who says there is no such thing as rape should be hauled out to a public place by three large perverts and buggered at high noon with all his clients watching.

b. The responsibility of the victim. The notion that rape is physically impossible is closely connected with perhaps the most prevalent and damaging opinion of all: that the onus of responsibility for sexual relations lies upon the woman. It is commonly believed that a man proposes and the woman disposes, by agreement or disagreement: if she gets raped, she has communicated badly, and it is her responsibility. She has made a mistake: she has led him on.

The concept is even found in the research literature on rape: Amir refers to certain rapes as 'victim precipitated'. The distinction is difficult to understand in relation to a crime whose basis is lack of consent to a specific activity, but its use by an academic is indicative of widespread socio-cultural assumptions about a woman's responsibility for what happens to her. These assumptions may be shared by the victim herself, and give rise to those feelings of guilt and self-blame, which form part of the aftermath of rape, and which are considered below.

Once again, however, the myth will be found to contain some traces of the truth. The issue of responsibility involves problems of cultural inheritance. Western society involves a degree of courtship and seduction between even the most consenting sexual partners, and sometimes that courtship and seduction will involve some ritual resistance. Misunderstanding of the difference between ritual and actual resistance can and does arise, and forms part of the experience of ordinary men and women.

These misunderstandings illustrate the fact that consent and responsibility for sexual relations are not straightforward concepts. It is vital that the assumption of general female responsibility is removed from investigative and judicial procedures, but it is also important that reform takes into account cultural inheritance and does not replace an old myth with a facile generalisation which ignores general human experience.

c. The motives of the attacker. Part of the familiar stereotype of the rapist is that he is a maniac. There is no factual support for this theory. Of rapists convicted in England and Wales in 1975, only 1.5 per cent were committed to psychiatric institutions: in 1980, this figure was 1.6 per cent (Home Ofice, 1976, 1981).

On the other hand, it appears to be assumed that if the rapist is not a maniac he is a normal man whose sexual desires are frustrated in some way and who, provoked by a woman 'leading him on', commits rape to release normal sexual tension. The research conducted by Nicholas Groth in his book *Men who rape* dispels this belief. In a study of convicted rapists, Groth found that they did not view the crime as primarily sexual. He states that the intent of the rapist 'is to hurt and degrade his victim. His weapon is sex' (Groth, 1978, p. 17).

> Rape is a Pseudosexual Act, a pattern of sexual behaviour that is concerned much more with status, hostility, control and dominance than with sensual pleasure or sexual satisfaction. It is sexual behaviour in the primary service of non-sexual needs (Groth, p. 13).

The results of Groth's research directly support the experience of many victims. Although the violation of rape concerns the sexual organs, and it invokes sexual taboos, many victims view the crime asexually, and respond to it mainly as a life-threatening situation. It

28 *The investigative context*

is very common for victims to state 'I thought he was going to kill me'.

If neither the victim nor the offender sees the crime as primarily sexual, then it is vital that the investigator does not. United States police departments have successfully included this concept in their training: during the field study, many officers expressed the opinion that rape was a crime of violence rather than of sex, and repeated with approval the remarks of Burgess and Holmstrom quoted at the beginning of this study.

The results of research: rape trauma syndrome

The victims of almost all crimes suffer some emotional or psychological reaction to it. This is particularly true in cases in which victims experience, or are threatened by, personal violence. The nature of human reaction to this or other forms of crisis have been under investigation by psychologists for some years. The initial work carried out by Lindemann in the 1940s has developed into an area of study known as 'crisis theory'. It has been found that the human reaction to crisis is predictable, and that techniques can be devised to assist the victims of crisis. These techniques may be of considerable importance to police and are discussed further in subsequent chapters. Following on from the work of Lindemann, Bard and Ellison (1974) have proposed that the elements of crisis to which victims react most strongly are its suddenness, arbitrariness and unpredictability—the 'Why me?' sensation—and that victims display helplessness and extreme suggestibility in the aftermath of crisis. These reactions, of course, depend upon the perceived severity of the crisis and the psychological and social resilience of the victim.

Rape is clearly a severe crisis and it could, therefore, be expected that these reactions would be found in its victims. In the 1970s, however, two researchers in Massachusetts set out to examine the possibility that victims of rape might experience symptoms particular to this offence. Burgess and Holmstrom found that, in addition to the general effects of crisis, victims of rape displayed a group of physical and psychological symptoms quite specific to this crime. They termed this group of symptoms rape trauma syndrome.

The work of Burgess and Holmstrom was based on a study of every victim of rape seen at a Boston hospital in a 12-month period during 1972 and 1973. They found that there were two specific phases of reaction to the crime. In the first few hours and days following an attack, victims experienced an acute reaction of disbelief and shock, compounded by physical trauma including bruising, soreness, and gastro-intestinal and genito-urinary disturbance. The victims expressed specific feelings concerning their attack—fear, humiliation and embarrassment, anger, desire for revenge and self-blame. Most interestingly, Burgess and Holmstrom found that victims reacted in almost equal proportions, either with crying, laughing and semi-hysterical behaviour, or with silent composure. This acute phase was followed by a period of integration and resolution, in which the victim tried to come to terms with the crime. Burgess and Holmstrom noted that during this period, victims altered their life styles, often changing their address, their job or their social network. Victims reported recurrent nightmares and phobias: emotional and sexual relationships with significant other persons were interrupted or damaged (Burgess and Holmstrom, 1974).

Although work carried out in relation to the victims of other crimes (Bard and Sangrey, 1979) suggests that the victims of all serious crimes suffer from a variety of unpleasant reactions, it is clear that the symptoms displayed by rape victims are both more severe and more predictable. The explanation appears to be that, in rape victimisation, normal crisis reactions are compounded by the taboos surrounding sexuality and the conflict created by the mythology outlined above, so that guilt, shame and self-blame keep emerging. Burgess and Holmstrom, for instance, note a case in which a woman was surprised by an unknown assailant in the hallway of her apartment block and was forced inside her own flat and raped. Despite fighting back to the extent of taking a knife off the assailant and being severely beaten, she said of the rape:

> I keep wondering maybe if I had done something different when I first saw him that it wouldn't have happened—neither he nor I would be in trouble. Maybe it was my fault. My father always said whatever a man did to a woman, she provoked it (Burgess and Holmstrom, p. 983).

Rape victims appear to exhibit another particular characteristic. It is widely known that feelings of guilt and shame may prevent some victims of rape from reporting the crime, but it is now becoming clear that, because of these feelings, the actual decision to report or not becomes part of the trauma. The American researchers Weis and Borges note:

> The trauma following a rape experience often revolves around the resolution of emotional conflicts connected with the decision of whether or not to report the rape (1975).

Although the findings of Burgess and Holmstrom suggest that the symptoms and reactions described are observable in all victims of rape, their severity is variable: they are likely to be increased by the perceived social distance between the victim and offender and, paradoxically, by the closeness of any personal relationship between them. Ability to overcome the crisis also depends upon the personal resilience of the individual, the support she can draw from her personal social network and the manner in which she is treated as the victim. Where a victim already suffers from psychiatric disturbance, Burgess and Holmstrom found that the effect of rape trauma syndrome could be devastating.

Little appears to be known about rape trauma syndrome in the United Kingdom. A computer search of all medical literature from 1974 found only a single reference to it in a British medical publication (Draper, 1983), although it is mentioned in the recommendations made by the London Rape Crisis Centre to the Royal Commission on Criminal Procedure (London Rape Crisis Centre, 1978b). In the United States, however, the syndrome has become part of the corpus of psychiatric knowledge, and psychiatrists have testified for the prosecution to the effect that rape trauma syndrome is a known condition, that a particular victim is suffering from it, and that therefore she must have been raped.

If the theory of rape trauma syndrome is accepted, then it must be significant to police. During police interviews, victims will be suffering from the series of reactions described by Burgess and Holmstrom as the acute phase of the syndrome. As they await trial and at trial, they will be suffering from the symptoms involved in the longer term phase.[4] Throughout the period of trauma, rape victims will also display the suggestibility and helplessness which appear in all victims of crisis. Because the decision whether or not to report the crime is of major psychological significance to victims, the manner in which they are treated by police as a consequence of that decision will have a major impact on the severity of the trauma they may suffer. If police treatment reinforces or reduces feelings of guilt and self-blame, it is likely to affect the ability of the witness to provide evidence and her effectiveness in doing so. Police administrators and senior investigators across the United States have accepted these arguments and have incorporated them into the training and work patterns of sex investigation units.

The discovery of a rape trauma syndrome is also significant because it has given medical validity to the special treatment of rape victims demanded by the women's movement. Establishing the validity of rape trauma syndrome as a psychological condition suffered exclusively by rape victims and having considerable impact upon their social network provided justification for the setting up of special centres to deal with such victims. Known as rape crisis centres, these facilities are important features of the context in which United States police departments operate.

Rape crisis centres in the United States and the United Kingdom

The existence of rape crisis centres is directly attributable to the earlier interest taken by the women's movement in the crime of rape. In the late 1960s and early 1970s, women concerned at the apparent failure of relevant law enforcement and medical agencies to cope adequately with the problems of rape victims, began to hold meetings where victims could discuss their feelings with fellow sufferers. At the same time as rape became an important issue in the United States, the nature of rape trauma syndrome and the benefits of socio-psychological counselling became apparent, and the idea of rape crisis centres became fashionable and appropriate. At first restricted to the great cities of the east, New York and Washington, 24-hour professional centres, with government funding provided as a result of pressure from the women's movement, began to appear all over the United States in the early 1970s. These centres have multiplied fast, and now almost every large city and many other communities have some form of centre specifically designed to provide this service. The survey *Forcible rape* found that, in 1977, 65 per cent of all communities and 95 per cent of large cities had special counselling services for the victims of rape (Vol. 1, p. 33). The pamphlet *Survivor* issued by the Los Angeles Police Department in conjunction with other agencies to all rape victims, lists 25 rape crisis centres in the Greater Los Angeles area.

The purpose of such centres has always been to provide psychological and social help for victims, to provide proper medical facilities in relation to pregnancy and venereal disease, and to provide such services on a 24-hour basis. Their counselling and advice services are not restricted to victims of rape alone, nor only to the victims of recent crime: they deal with the effects of all kinds of sexual abuse and sexual assault, and much of their work and much of their time are devoted to coping with long-term reactions to sexual violation.

These laudable aims have always been combined with fierce lobbying for the rights of victims to better treatment. Initially, these centres were organised by women, who were politically radical in United States terms and who freely expressed trenchant criticisms of both the establishment in general and of law enforcement agencies in particular. Chappell and Singer (1977) note, for example, that:

> Women's groups believe that the present treatment of rape victims by police represents one of the major deterrents to reporting of this crime, and to eliciting the further cooperation of those victims who complain officially they have been raped.

Russell (1975) expresses even more forceful criticisms:

> In general, the treatment of Ms Kelley by the police is another example of how the victim is treated as the criminal. In this case, she was tried by police whose incompetence and inefficiency were as noteworthy as their hostility.

As a result of this sort of criticism, the centres themselves and those who worked in them were regarded with antipathy and hostility by police, a state of affairs given prominence by professionals in both organisations and by the public media. This now appears to have changed. Table 3.3 presents the views of sex crimes detectives and police administrators canvassed in 1978 by the survey *Forcible rape* (Vol. 1, p. 33).

The author's own observations in the United States have confirmed these findings. Where rape crisis centres exist, local police have made every effort to co-operate with them, by meeting, listening and incorporating some of the centres' ideas into police procedures. The effect has been to enable both police and the crisis centres' staff to provide a more professional and integrated service to victims. The dialogue has resulted in police becoming more aware of the needs of victims, and rape crisis centres more understanding of the requirements of police procedures. As a result, for instance, rape crisis centre counsellors interviewed during this study would not normally insist on being present at police interviews and would allow the officer to exercise his judgement as to whether this would be in the interests of the victim. On the other hand, police officers appeared to be pleased that others could relieve them of the burden of providing emotional support to the victim in the aftermath of the crime and, where appropriate, during court processes.

Two further advantages have accrued to police. Liaison has not only enabled United States police departments to offer an enhanced service to the victims of rape, it has enabled them to be seen to do so. As described in Chapter 6, United States police departments have used every form of the media to publicise this kind of co-operation, and the resulting improvement in services to sexual assault victims, in order to enhance the public image of the department as a whole. Secondly, by showing themselves to be reasonable in their approach and receptive to fresh ideas, police departments have succeeded in establishing a workable compromise between the requirements of police operations and the more far-reaching demands of some of the early rape crisis activists. Clear demarcation lines have been established between the areas of interest of both parties, and, through dialogue and explanation as well as through change, much of the original criticism of the police handling of rape has been defused.

Table 3.3: View taken of rape crisis centres by police in the United States

		%
Where institution exists: found by police to be	Very co-operative	65
	Somewhat co-operative	32
	Not co-operative	3
Where institution does not exist: felt by police to be	Needed	98.5
	Not needed	1.5

In the United Kingdom, the situation is ostensibly different. In November 1983, there were only 22 rape crisis centres in England, none in Wales, three in Scotland and one in Northern Ireland (see Appendix B). Using the same broad categories as the American

34 *The investigative context*

survey *Forcible rape*, the 15 provincial police forces in whose police areas rape crisis centres are situated were asked to comment on the sort of co-operation they felt their local centre extended to police. The results are shown in Table 3.4 and, while this position is not as encouraging as that in the United States, it is not as bleak as might have been assumed.

Table 3.4: View taken of rape crisis centres by provincial police forces in the United Kingdom

		No.	%
Where institution	Very co-operative	3	26
exists: found by	Somewhat co-operative	8	57
police to be	Not co-operative	3	26

Note: The table not only excludes the Metropolitan Police but also one force which recorded different relationships with the two centres with which it had dealings.

Of the 22 rape crisis centres in existence in England, only those in London and Birmingham provide a 24-hour service. The West Midlands Police responded to the questionnaire by noting that the relationship between the police and the two rape crisis centres within its boundaries was 'very co-operative'. Although there have been difficulties, a working relationship has been established and some mutual training undertaken. West Midlands Police Force Orders direct officers to inform rape victims of the existence of the centres, and allow officers discretion to permit representatives of the centre to accompany victims during police procedures.

The relationship of the Metropolitan Police and the London Rape Crisis Centre is very different. As might be expected, the London centre deals with more cases than any other, has been in existence longer, and has adopted or had forced upon it the role of principal voice in the United Kingdom rape crisis centre movement. Possibly as a result, and in common with its early American counterparts, it has been stridently and persistently critical of rape investigation in the Metropolitan Police area, and at present will not enter into dialogue with police. Staff at the London centre would not, for example, agree to be interviewed as part of this study.[5] For its part, the Metropolitan Police has not officially acknowledged the validity of the centre's services and, at present, does not officially refer victims to the centre, preferring to direct them to the National

Health Service, Social Services Departments or, increasingly, to local branches of the victim support schemes.

Outside Birmingham and London, the principal restrictions on rape crisis centres arise because of lack of funding: there are few of them and they do not operate a 24-hour service. Responses to the questionnaire sent to police forces indicated that it was the restricted availability of the centres, and a perceived lack of experience among volunteer staff, that principally inhibited police referrals.

It may be that the pattern of development witnessed in the United States will occur here, and the number of professionally staffed rape crisis centres will increase. If this is so, then it is likely that the American pattern of initial hostility followed by active liaison and co-operation will be repeated both in the Metropolitan Police District and in other force areas. Two factors, however, are likely to make growth in the rape crisis centre movement in Britain much more gradual than in the United States. First, in the United Kingdom there are very few of the kind of higher education courses in crisis and paramedical or social counselling which provide the better rape crisis centres in the United States with staff. In the United Kingdom, counselling is either an experiential skill developed by practitioners in medical and social fields, who are unlikely to leave their secure professions to join the staff of rape crisis centres, or a scarce and expensive professional resource. This situation has been created by the cost, length and limited availability of private psychotherapy training courses. The second inhibitor is lack of funds: the growth of the rape crisis centre movement in the United States coincided with a period of increasing prosperity leading to increased investment in community projects, and centres were set up with generous support from public funds. In Britain, rape crisis centres are now competing for a share of a diminishing pool of charitable and governmental funds. While existing centres are likely to continue to be supported, additional 24-hour centres may find finance difficult to obtain.

Both of these factors make it likely that improvement in aftercare for rape victims will depend upon the development of victim support schemes. Their umbrella organisation, the National Association of Victims Support Schemes, receives considerable financial support from government, while the low overheads of individual schemes enable them to obtain necessary funds from local government or local charitable sources. The schemes are usually closely linked to existing social agencies, and have access to trained personnel from different specialisms.

Medical services for victims

The British idea of the regularly employed but independent police surgeon is not familiar in the United States, where persons in custody and witnesses are examined either by doctors at central gaols, or by casualty units. Rape victims are examined not by police surgeons in police stations, but at general hospitals or at the surgeries of individual doctors.

The quality of service and the methods used by medical practitioners on the two sides of the Atlantic lie outside the scope of this study, but the difference between the locations of the examination is not only reflected in all American literature on rape and its investigation, but is also symbolic of the radically different or 'new' approach to the treatment of rape victims currently practised in the United States. An examination of the role of the police needs to take this into account.

Despite a tentative reference to hospitals in the 1983 Home Office Circular on rape investigation, the examination of rape victims in hospital casualty units is viewed with considerable disfavour by most police surgeons in Britain and, in particular, by the Association of Police Surgeons of Great Britain.[6] It is argued that a rape victim becomes only one more type of casualty in a possibly understaffed and overworked emergency department. It is difficult to prevent non-specialised staff from taking immediate remedial medical action which may destroy evidence, and it appears to be difficult to maintain confidentiality in the open-plan environment of many casualty departments. The same problems were well known in the United States at the beginning of the campaign to improve the treatment of rape victims there. In *The victim of rape: institutional reactions*, a sequel to their first study, Holmstrom and Burgess examined the treatment of rape victims by the institutions and bureaucracies with which they came into contact. It was apparently common to fail to segregate rape victims from other patients while waiting, to call out into a crowded waiting room for the rape victim to identify herself, and to leave the victim alone and partially dressed for long periods of time while awaiting examination. There was a lack of forensic training for doctors performing examinations, and a reluctance on their part to testify in court.

In large part, these problems have been overcome; most jurisdictions now use only a selected hospital or hospitals for the examination of rape victims, and hospitals have established a confidential and effective medical protocol for such cases. Nursing and medical staff now undergo training in forensic examination, and doctors have been persuaded of the necessity and desirability of court attendances. Many hospitals now use 'rape kits'.

The efficient use of hospitals for examining victims allows American doctors to offer a radically different service from that offered by police surgeons in the United Kingdom because the rape victim is seen as a patient in much more complete terms. In the course of an examination in Britain, a police surgeon will take note of injuries, give advice as to first aid, and make recommendations as to future treatment; where necessary, he will recommend immediate hospitalisation and take any steps necessary to preserve the health of the patient. However, his primary role remains the collection of evidence of penetration and/or consent. His examination room, in a police station or elsewhere, is not equipped for full gynaecological examination and he will normally prescribe drugs neither for the termination of pregnancy nor to prevent venereal disease. He will not usually become involved in counselling about the emotional or psychological after-effects of the crime.

Practice in the United States is entirely different. Emphasis is placed upon a full gynaecological examination, almost invariably with the aid of a speculum in the lithotomy position. Full notes are taken as to sexual and menstrual history, and the victim is given information about the likelihood of conception and the effects of a termination of pregnancy by menstrual extraction, by an IUD or by high-dosage oestrogen. A serology sample to detect venereal disease is also taken, and an anti-venereal disease medication is given. The doctor and nurses will be in contact with a local rape crisis centre, will be aware of whatever counselling and therapeutic services are available and will advise the patient accordingly. An information leaflet for the patient, prepared by the Sexual Trauma Services, San Francisco, is attached as Appendix C.

These procedures have been discussed at length with the Honorary Secretary of the Association of Police Surgeons of Great Britain, and with other police surgeons practising in London. While they have been in general agreement with the above findings, the police surgeons interviewed have made the following observations. The question of examination in the lithotomy position with a speculum is a matter of debate and individual practice among police surgeons, many of whom feel it represents too great a further trauma for the patient. It can also be argued that its insertion may push material of evidential value into the vagina, thereby damaging the value of evidence obtained. Some surgeons, however, do use the instruments and they are included in some 'sexual offence kits'. Collection of evidence of venereal disease requires separate types of swabs (charcoal), which must be handled differently to other swabs: no forensic laboratory in the United Kingdom has bacteriologists, and such samples would have to be forwarded to venereal disease clinics. Under these circumstances, police surgeons do not see the collection of such samples as appropriate to their role. A leaflet giving information to the patient (at Appendix D) has been prepared by the Association of Police Surgeons of Great Britain, and is gradually being brought into use. As well as providing the patient with a certain amount of information about the role of the police surgeon, this leaflet also forms a confidential note to the patient's own practitioner and to the local venereal disease clinic. The Metropolitan Police are currently negotiating with a number of general hospitals in London with the eventual aim of providing a confidential service to rape victims.

While there is no doubt that police surgeons in Britain generally carry out their necessarily limited duties in a highly professional manner, the effect is that rape victims are treated in isolation from other branches of the medical profession. The police surgeon is not required, although some do, to follow up the progress of the victim, and he does not seek to deal with the major issues of pregnancy and venereal infection that will be alarming her. Further difficulty is caused by the shortage of female police surgeons (whose recruitment was recommended in the 1983 Home Office Circular) and the fact that only half of the doctors who work for the police are members of the Association of Police Surgeons of Great Britain. Although training in rape examination is given by the Association, there is undoubtedly scope for extending that training to all doctors who work for the police, or for restricting rape examinations only to certain specially trained police surgeons.

In the United States the medical treatment of the victim is all embracing: she is counselled and reassured against the twin fears of pregnancy and venereal disease, and the same medical team will continue to look after her. This approach is reflected in the standard medical report used across the United States, which deals with the general condition of the victim, pulse, temperature, etc., the offences outlined, the treatment given and the dates of follow-up examination. It also includes an excellent diagram for the indication of injuries. (Such a diagram is currently being considered by chief officers of police in Britain; it will, if introduced, represent a considerable improvement over current practice.) The effect of this all-inclusive medical attention is of great significance for the investigator: the victim feels herself supported by state agencies, and the detective therefore meets a victim who is medically reassured and able to concentrate fully on giving evidence. As a result, the task of the investigator may be made much easier.

Notes

1. *Miranda v Arizona* 384 US 436 (1966) established the rights of persons in custody to be warned, amongst other things, of their right to remain silent and to consult with and have counsel present during questioning.
2. Verbal estimate by an official of the Law Enforcement Assistance Administration to the author, 1982.
3. The activity of American media in 1984 in relation to the Big Dan's Tavern case indicates, however, that American legislation designed to control newspapers and radio is not fully effective in relation to television. In the United Kingdom, the filming of any trial, let alone a rape trial, is prohibited by law, and the naming of the complainant as it occurred in the 'Big Dan' case would be highly unlikely.
4. Shapland's observations in her study *The victim in the criminal justice system* (1981) suggest that feelings of insecurity and uneasiness during court processes are particularly noticeable in the case of victims of rape.
5. They were, however, willing to provide answers to specific questions by telephone. It was stressed that staff at the London Rape Crisis Centre would respond to an official approach by the Metropolitan Police. They themselves did not expect to make any further overtures for official recognition.
6. Personal communication.

4 AMERICAN POLICE DEPARTMENTS: FOUR CASE STUDIES

Newark

The Police Department of Newark employs just over 1,000 officers, and serves a population of 250,000. The city of Newark was one of the cities most affected by the serious civil disorders of 1967-8. It remains an area of severe urban deprivation and, although much civic rebuilding has occurred, the population is housed in mainly poor and overcrowded conditions.

The Sexual Assault and Rape Analysis Unit (SARA) was established in 1975, as a result of a federal grant. In 1982, the Unit consisted of a lieutenant, two sergeants and six detectives. It deals with all sexual offences from indecent exposure and 'peeping Toms' to rape, but excludes homicide and all vice and morals cases. Sexual molestation of children is dealt with by detectives of the Unit in liaison with detectives from the city's Juvenile Division. As was the case with the other police departments studied, the SARA Unit was regarded as one of the most prestigious units in which a detective could work.

An indication of the workload of the SARA Unit is given in Table 4.1. Of the 671 cases in 1981, 646 (96 per cent) were offences of sexual assault; of these, the SARA Unit cleared 266 cases (41 per cent).

Table 4.1: Sexual offences investigated by the SARA Unit, Newark Police Department, 1975–1981

Year	No.	Year on year % change
1975	398a	
1976	465	+17
1977	489	+ 5
1978	400	−18
1979	504	+26
1980	609	+21
1981	671	+10

Note: a. Estimated from six months' figures.
Source: Statistics supplied by Newark Police Department.

Of the seven operational detectives in Newark (excluding the lieutenant and one sergeant), at least one officer works in the evening, and one officer at night. Either before or shortly after their transfer to the Unit, all officers are sent on a four-day sexual investigation course held by the New Jersey State Police. This course includes training on evidence gathering, interview techniques appropriate to children and adults, attitudinal training, a description of rape trauma syndrome and an introduction to the principles of forensic and biochemical evidence.

All rape victims in Newark are examined at one hospital, the United Hospitals Medical Centre. The staff have received training in the forensic examination of victims, and operate a strict protocol. Rape victims are always referred to as 'Case R Patients' and a sexual offences kit is used. Victims are given advice and preventive treatment for pregnancy and sexually-transmitted disease and a hospital social worker trained in socio-psychological counselling attempts to maintain contact with all victims. All prosecutions for sexual offences are conducted by a single prosecutor in the Office of the Essex County District Attorney, and regular contact is maintained between medical, prosecutorial and police staffs, all of whom participate in mutual training.

New York

New York was chosen as a field site for this study because of the high prestige of its innovative anti-rape programmes and its high incidence of rape. Because of pressure of time, the interviews carried out in New York were less complete than in other cities, but there remains no doubt that, while the will remains, the ability of the police department to tackle rape has been severely curtailed in recent years. The influence of the women's movement was especially marked in New York and, faced with pressure from women's groups following a 37 per cent increase in the reported rate of forcible rape in 1972 over 1971, the New York Police Department established an all-female sex crimes unit in December 1972. This central unit of 18 officers was given the task of investigating all sex crimes in New York, and within weeks was overwhelmed. The Police Department then established five further teams of male and female officers in different boroughs of the city, and the all-female unit was transformed into a crimes analysis unit.

Officers from this unit maintained computerised *modus operandi* files, provided additional female detective assistance to the borough detectives, and established a 24-hour crisis hot line, constantly operated by female detectives. This hot line provided referral to appropriate area investigators or to supportive agencies. The Sex Crimes Analysis Unit produced an annual *Overview*, which in 1978 reviewed the development of sexual offence investigation and the Unit's involvement in different activities, including publicity drives, liaison with the Mayor's Task Force on Rape, workshops on psychological intervention and sensitivity training for police officers.

By 1982, this situation had entirely changed. The Sex Crimes Analysis Unit at New York Police Headquarters by then consisted of only one officer and the majority of its functions had been discontinued. A team of female officers, however, still operated the hot line. A Sex Crimes Investigation Unit in one part of the city, which was observed for this study, had consisted of 18 detectives in 1974, but in 1982 had a staff of only eight officers, who were responsible for the investigation of all sexual crime and all child abuse within their area. In addition to the rest of their caseload, these eight officers apparently had investigated more than 1,000 forcible rapes in 1981. Despite their original pride in belonging to a Sex Crimes Investigation Unit, the detectives interviewed were demoralised, cynical and entirely overwhelmed by the volume of crime. Although they had undergone intensive sensitivity training in the past, courses or seminars were now infrequent and insufficient time was granted for attendance. Personnel leaving Sex Crimes Investigation Units were apparently infrequently replaced, and the direct impression both from the police and others was that the political impetus to solve the problem of rape in New York City had been lost.

The explanation for this situation lies in the financial restrictions being imposed upon the New York Police Department, although Sex Crimes Units have fared better than some other specialised squads. Whatever the current state of these squads, the Sex Crimes Investigation and Analysis Units of the New York Police Department exercised a seminal influence over other jurisdictions, and many of their methods have been adopted by other police departments across the United States. Two of the officers involved in the inauguration of the Units, Lieutenant Mary Keefe and Sergeant Harry O'Reilly, have now left the Police Department, and teach those methods in colleges and universities, Harry O'Reilly being an Adjunct Professor at the John Jay College of Criminal Justice, New York.

In addition to the financial problems of the city, a consideration of the *Overview* mentioned above and conversations with operational detectives suggest that the New York sex crimes investigation system grew over-complex and that this also contributed to its decline.

San Francisco

San Francisco Police Department employs just over 2,500 police officers to serve a population of 850,000 in a small contained area of 49 square miles. San Francisco is a rich city, with a population of mixed racial background, and now has one of the largest and most politically powerful homosexual subcultures in the world. The Police Department maintains only a Central Detective Bureau, and the Sex Crimes Detail has been in existence for many years: in the last decade it has been enlarged and in 1982 it consisted of nine detectives and one lieutenant. Table 4.2 gives details of rapes and other serious sexual assaults investigated by the unit, which is also responsible for lesser offences such as indecent exposure and obscene telephone calls.

Table 4.2: Cases of sexual assault investigated by the Sex Crimes Detail, San Francisco Police Department, 1980–1982

	1980	1981	% change	1982	% change
Rape	535	487	− 9	502	+ 3
Attempted rape	209	200	− 4	223	+ 12
Sodomy	46	48	+ 4	38	− 21
Oral copulation	48	65	+ 35	84	+ 29
Total	838	800	− 5	847	+ 6

Source: Statistics supplied by the San Francisco Police Department.

Once again, the Sex Crimes Detail is held in high repute within the Police Department. Officers on the unit are drawn from other central detective units and have, in many cases, served for some years with the Sex Crimes Detail. Officers work office hours but one officer is on call for the rest of the evening and at night. He may call upon another nominated officer for assistance.

Officers seem to receive little formal training in sex crimes investigation but are trained on the job by working alongside more experienced officers. Equally important, they work very closely with the deputy district attorneys and with medical personnel.

The office of the district attorney has a staff of four prosecutors who deal exclusively with sexual crime. The district attorney has recognised that sexual offences present very difficult problems for the prosecutor, and has ensured that the staff involved have considerable experience. Despite this experience and the close liaison that exists with police, the conservative nature of prosecution decisions in rape cases mentioned in Chapter 3 is reflected in prosecution statistics for San Francisco: in 1981 the San Francisco district attorney refused to prosecute in 85 out of the 349 cases of rape (24 per cent) for which persons were arrested.

The most notable feature of rape investigation in San Francisco is the existence of a Central Emergency Unit to deal exclusively with the victims of sexual assault. Funded by the San Francisco Department of Public Health, the Sexual Trauma Service is open 24 hours a day, every day. It provides an examining room for treatment and forensic examination. Victims also receive treatment and advice on pregnancy and sexually-transmitted infection. The service provides socio-psychological counselling and a regular follow-up procedure. It deals with about 650 cases a year from all over the hinterland of San Francisco, and arranges an average of seven counselling sessions with each victim. It makes stringent efforts to maintain contact with all victims in the weeks after an assault, and it refers victims on to longer-term psychological assistance if required.

The Sexual Trauma Service receives the full co-operation of the San Francisco Police Department, which brings all victims of rape to its premises for examination. There is direct, confidential consultation between the Sexual Trauma Service and the detectives of the Sex Crimes Detail, who normally interview the victim after she has received initial counselling from the Sexual Trauma Service. If a victim wishes, staff from the Sexual Trauma Service will accompany her through police interviews, although they do not encourage this. More importantly, Sexual Trauma Service staff often accompany victims through court procedures.

Since its inauguration, liaison between the Sexual Trauma Service and the Sex Crimes Detail has provided an excellent service to the victims of rape. Victims who had been seen by the staff of both institutions were interviewed and observed during this study and their calm and collected state was apparent. They gave accounts of the dignity and professional treatment that had been accorded to them. It is also significant that the excellence of the Sexual Trauma Service seems to have had a beneficial effect on the reputation of the San Francisco Police Department. Prior to the existence of the Sexual Trauma Service, much had been made of alleged inadequacies in police investigation by groups like Bay Area Women Against Rape. In the face of the professional service now provided, this criticism has been largely dispelled.

Los Angeles

The Los Angeles Police Department employs approximately 7,000 officers covering a huge area of the County of Greater Los Angeles. It is divided into 17 precinct areas, in each of which there is a team of sex crimes investigators between two and four strong. There is a Central Rape Unit, which has a crime analysis function and coordinates the activities of the precinct units. If a large-scale operation is necessary, the central unit can be expanded to form a central investigative team. Offences against children and organised child pornography are dealt with by separate central units. Training of sex investigators is carried out at the Los Angeles Police Academy in conjunction with the Central Rape Unit, under the direction of the Police Department's psychologist.

The office of the district attorney maintains a prosecution team dedicated to sexual offences. The relationship between the deputy district attorneys and the police seems cordial and effective. Because of the geographical distribution of the police area, no central hospital or hospitals are designated for rape victims, but the Los Angeles Police Department has co-operated in the production of a full protocol for hospital staff.

The Department has also pursued a policy of active co-operation with a considerable number of external agencies concerned with sexual assault. For instance, the booklet *Survivor* (extract at Appendix A), published by the Los Angeles Commission on Assaults Against Women, is given to all victims of sexual assault by the Los Angeles Police Department and the Department co-operates with all the numerous women's organisations listed in its pages.

Among the many rape crisis centres operating in the Greater Los

Angeles area, the most prestigious is probably the Rape Treatment Center at Santa Monica, where victims receive treatment equal to the services provided by the Sexual Trauma Service in San Francisco. The Rape Treatment Center, however, specialises in long-term socio-psychological counselling. During recent years it has been highly influential in focusing attention on the issue of sexual assault.

Unfortunately, the history of official rape investigation in Los Angeles has followed a similar pattern to that in New York. Once the predominant police issue in Los Angeles, rape is no longer the primary concern of women's pressure groups, who have now taken up the cause of domestic violence. The Central Rape Unit has been cut from eight staff to three, and has been redesignated the Rape and Domestic Violence Unit. Consequently, the crime analysis function is no longer effective and precinct detectives receive little information about crime patterns affecting their area. Despite this, through thorough training of their detectives and extensive co-operation with other agencies, the Los Angeles Police Department appears to be able to offer an effective service to the victims of rape within its police area, of whom there were 2,705 in 1981 and 2,757 in 1982. Interviews with victims in the process of investigation indicated a high level of satisfaction with their treatment by police. It was noticeable that the Los Angeles Police Department, which receives a generally unfavourable press, attracts little criticism over its handling of sexual assault investigation.

Summary

The four police departments involved in this study are all responsible for inner-city areas of dense population with high overall crime rates and a high incidence of rape. The size of all the forces studied and the complexity of their internal organisation parallels that of similar metropolitan forces in the United Kingdom.[1] Each department maintains a specialist sexual offence investigation unit which was set up in response to political pressure from the women's movement about a decade ago. Since their inauguration, the largest of these squads, in New York and Los Angeles, have developed and declined in a way which closely parallels the development and decline of rape as a specific political issue. In each city the police department has established effective liaison with medical and counselling services, and has apparently received more favourable media comment as a result.

Sexual assault investigation in these departments is generally characterised by:

> The restriction of sexual offence investigation to dedicated teams.
> The selection and special training of officers for sexual offence investigation.
> High prestige for the sexual offences unit.
> Special working relationships with the office of the local district attorney.
> Extensive collaboration with external centres for the treatment and aftercare of victims.

These are the external and organisational features which mark this kind of advanced unit. Even more fundamental to them are the changed investigative techniques which they apply. These are outlined in Chapter 6, following a review of the problems presented by sexual offence investigation.

Note

1. The Metropolitan Police has an establishment of 27,000 officers, the West Midlands Police an establishment of 7,000 and the Merseyside Police an establishment of 4,500.

5 THE PROBLEMS OF SEXUAL OFFENCE INVESTIGATION

The problems involved in the investigation of the crime of rape are generally the same in the United States as in the United Kingdom. They may be divided into those common to most crimes against the person and those unique to sex crimes investigation. It is important to emphasise that American initiatives are not startling developments. Practice in the United States has steadily diverged from British practice by a gradual change in police attitudes to and knowledge of the crime and its victims.

United States police departments are faced with a much higher incidence of sexual crime than are police forces in the United Kingdom (see Chapter 2). There is also a much higher incidence in the United States of repeater or recidivist rape. Americans use the term 'hot prowl' rape for that type of rape which occurs when an unknown assailant breaks in or forces his way into the premises of the victim. Hot prowl rapes form a higher proportion of all rapes in the United States than they do in the United Kingdom.

Investigative problems common to crimes against the person

Investigative problems common to crimes against the person concern the collection and interpretation of forensic evidence and the identification of the unknown assailant.

Forensic evidence

Although the type of samples may differ, the requirement to obtain forensic evidence is the same in cases of rape as in many other crimes. Investigators of rape need an understanding of the methods of evidence gathering, the significance of various samples and the techniques available to laboratory technicians. The desirability of effective forensic examination is understood equally on both sides of the Atlantic. However, the geographic dispersal of law enforcement agencies in the United States and the different ways in which they are financed has led to a parallel fragmentation of forensic laboratory expertise. In San Francisco, for instance, blood, clothing bearing seminal staining and other clothing from the same rape investigation might have to be examined in three different laboratories. There is, therefore, no suggestion that the standards of forensic expertise currently available in the United Kingdom are in any way inferior to those existing in the United States.

Identification of the unknown assailant

Forcible rape found that fewer than 25 per cent of victims were able to name their assailants immediately (Vol. 1, p. 24). The identification of the unknown assailant, therefore, remains a vital part of detective duties. Table 5.1 describes the identification methods used by United States police departments and the success of those methods.

Table 5.1: Methods used by United States police departments to identify unknown assailants and the success of those methods

Method	Per cent of cases in which each method used	Per cent of cases in which each method identified suspect (N=1,259)	Success rate
	%	%	%
'Mug shots'	31	9	29
Fingerprints	14	2	14
Line-up	10	6	60
Suspects' belongings	8	2	25
Modus operandi	7	2	29
Stolen property	6	2	33
Unusual characteristics	6	0.7	12
Vehicle licence no.	5	5	100
Informant	0.4	0.1	25

Source: *Forcible rape*, Vol. IX, pp. 41–2.

All these methods are well known in Britain. Three of them, however, are used differently in the United States. The use of mug shots or photograph albums appears less constrained by procedural rules. There is no prohibition on the maintenance of albums specifically for sex offenders. Albums may also be constructed on the basis of race and age groupings. Where a particular individual is suspected his photograph can be placed with only three or four others rather than the 12 required in England and Wales. Most important of all, in many states, all persons convicted of any sexual offence must register with police and it is therefore in theory easier to trace suspects, although the discrepancy in the size of the United States and the United Kingdom makes comparison impossible. A system of grouping photographs by type of offence used to be practised in the witness albums section maintained at New Scotland Yard. However, in 1968 this practice was discontinued, apparently on the advice of the Home Office and the Lord Chancellor's Department. The workings of the witness album section are currently being examined by the Metropolitan Police but there is no suggestion that offence groups will be re-created.

Identification parades or line-ups are also more streamlined in the United States. Rather than the eight required in the United Kingdom, no more than five other persons are required to parade with the suspect. Much more significantly, the victim is able to view the parade and identify the suspect without being seen by the persons on parade. The rights of the suspect are protected by the presence of an attorney or independent observer.

Lastly, many areas of the United States use computers to operate *modus operandi* files. While this is an expensive and time-consuming process, and is of direct relevance only to the pursuit of repeater or recidivist rapists, it also provides an invaluable data base which can be used to increase knowledge and understanding of the way in which rapists operate. All police departments have developed detailed questionnaires for officers to complete in connection with sexual crimes. These are normally used to create a computerised data base enabling neighbouring sex crimes units to share criminal intelligence, including details of methods used and persons in custody and under suspicion.

In the United Kingdom, the Metropolitan Police has begun a fairly simple computerised sexual assault index. this index, together with an enhanced version of crime pattern analysis being tested at New Scotland Yard, should begin to provide police in the South-East of England with information about repeat offenders and enable them to compare forensic evidence of cases believed to be linked. This system is still in its infancy, but once fully developed, is expected to improve the effectiveness of rape investigation. Other likely advances within the Metropolitan Police are the early introduction of a complete computerised crime report system which would considerably extend the current availability of information. The possibility of psychological profiling techniques for the identification of rape suspects is also currently being examined.

The problems of sexual offence investigation 51

The advanced information systems in use in the United States may, therefore, appear in the United Kingdom but changes in legislation and practice concerning the use of photographs and identification parades would be necessary before police in the United Kingdom could begin to solve the 15 per cent of cases through mug shots and line-ups described in Table 5.1.

Major reform is unlikely given the weight of evidence concerning eye-witness testimony (for example, Clifford and Bull, 1978). However, there may be growing support for the introduction of identification parades in which the suspect cannot see the victim. This system is currently under test in Scotland. A Scotland Yard working party considering the administrative arrangements for identification parades is also examining the possibility of approaching the Home Office for authority to conduct experiments with this form of identification parade.

Investigative problems specifically associated with sexual offences

There appear to be four areas of difficulty unique to the investigation of sexual crimes. While they are all interconnected they can usefully be separated into the issues of failure to report offences; false reporting; withdrawal of complaint after report; and the question of consent. The United States police departments which were visited have accepted that all four of these issues are of major relevance to the methods they use in interviewing victims, training police officers and liaising with non-police bodies, and to publicity.

Non-reporting of offences

It is a commonplace of policing that police receive reports of only a proportion of crime and that the 'dark' volume of crime is greater than that reported. Rape, however, is in a special category. The compilers of the Federal Bureau of Investigation's crime statistics for the United States 1982 state that forcible rape:

> . . . is still recognised as one of the most under-reported of all Index Crimes. Victims' fear of their assailants and their embarrassment over the incidents are just two factors which can affect their decisions to contact law enforcement. (Federal Bureau of Investigation, 1983, p. 14).

52 The problems of sexual offence investigation

There is some statistical evidence to support this thesis. In its study, *The challenge of crime in a free society*, the United States Presidential Commission on Law Enforcement and the Administration of Justice commissioned the National Opinion Research Centre (NORC) of the University of Chicago to conduct a survey of 100,000 households into actual and reported rates of crime. The comparison between the rates of crime reported by households and the officially reported rates for the same period in the Uniform Crime Reports (UCR) is given in Table 5.2.

Table 5.2: Comparison of actual and reported crime rates in the United States

	NORC1965–6 (per 100,000)	UCR1966	Per cent reported occurring
Forcible rape	42.5	12.2	28.7
Robbery	94.0	61.4	65.2
Aggravated assault	218.3	106.6	48.5

Source: President's Commission on Law Enforcement and the Administration of Justice, *The challenge of crime in a free society*, 1967, p. 22.

The more recent United States National Crime Survey of 1979 estimated that only 50 per cent of forcible rapes were reported to police (US Department of Justice, 1981). By August 1978, of the 500 persons who had reported an attack to the rape crisis centre in London, only just over half had reported it to the police (London Rape Crisis Centre, 1978a). In 1980, 39.8 per cent of women reporting a rape to the Birmingham Rape Crisis Centre had not reported it to the police (Birmingham Rape Crisis Centre, 1981). (No figures are available on the number of women in these cities who reported attacks neither to the centres nor to the police.) The *British crime survey*, published in 1982 and concerned with the relationship between reported and actual crime levels, records only one rape-related case reported to its compilers but not to police (Hough and Mayhew, p. 21). The authors of the report of the survey concede, however, that its methods of data gathering were not likely to elicit information concerning sexual crime.

Reasons for the non-reporting of rape are difficult to document. The research carried out in the United States, for instance by Schultz and the San Francisco Sexual Trauma Service and in the United Kingdom by the Rape Counselling and Research Project and Chambers and Millar, indicate that conflicting pressures affect the victim's decision to report. In addition to normal responses to criminal victimisation, such as desire for justice, the principal pressure in favour of reporting appears to be the thought that not to do so will leave the rapist free to rape and possibly kill another woman or a child. The pressures against reporting are those of embarrassment, a fear of retaliation and a fear of poor treatment by police.

United States police departments have accepted that the non-reporting of rape, although not reflected in crime statistics, results in a serious failure on their part to detect crime. They have recognised that the pressures against reporting can be affected by police action and have taken steps to change police procedures to mitigate these pressures. In addition, some of the police departments run publicity campaigns to encourage reporting—the slogan 'Silence Frees a Rapist' was used by the Newark Police Department in such a campaign in 1982. It is similarly the stated policy of all police forces in the United Kingdom to encourage the official reporting of all crime. It may be, however, that more resources could be used to encourage increased reporting of rape, as in the United States. Rape which is not reported cannot be detected.

False reporting and the withdrawal of complaints

The issue of false allegations of sexual assault is particularly important to any study of police procedures in relation to the investigation of rape. Legal procedure on both sides of the Atlantic has long operated on the basis of the possibility of false evidence being given by complainants (see Wigmore, 1970; Archbold, 1982; Marsh *et al.*, 1982; and Temkin, 1982). Similarly, instructional literature for detectives has traditionally assumed that questionable allegations are more numerous and a cause of greater difficulty and concern in rape cases than in other criminal investigations. Even the fifteenth report of the Criminal Law Revision Committee notes that 'By no means every accusation of rape is true' (paragraph 2.7).

The New York Sex Crimes Analysis Unit noted that only 2 per cent of the rapes reported in their first year of operation were false (Chappell, Geis and Geis, p. 18). A number of studies, including Brownmiller (p. 366), indicate, without clear authority, that this 2 per cent rate is the same as that for other categories of crime. In 1982, 5.8 per cent of all crimes known to police in England and Wales were estimated as being officially classified 'no-crime' (Chartered Institute of Public Finance and Accountancy). Yet there is considerable evidence that investigators in the United

States (historically) and in the United Kingdom (currently) seem prepared to give serious consideration to the proposition that between 50 per cent and 70 per cent of all allegations of rape are false (See Csida and Csida, p. 18; Brownmiller, p. 365; Firth; and Chambers and Millar, pp. 85ff). The disparity between these figures warrants further examination.

A report of rape can be false in only three circumstances. First, the report can be made out of malice or mental derangement when no sexual act has occurred. In these cases there will be little or no corroborative evidence. Secondly, a woman who has been raped can make a false identification of the rapist in good faith: such cases place the burden of resolution upon the criminal justice system. Lastly and most problematic are the instances where consensual sexual intercourse has occurred between the defendant and the complainant, who later decides to make a complaint of rape. Although this possibility has to be acknowledged, the embarrassment and discomfort of investigation, medical examination and trial make it most unlikely that considerable numbers of women will make false reports where consensual intercourse has occurred.

If the above arguments are accepted, then there can be no credible basis for the suggestion that 70 per cent, 50 per cent or even 20 per cent of allegations of sexual assault are false, in the sense of untrue. It is more likely that this perceived false report rate derives from some assumption made by the investigator or created by the procedures he has to operate. It lies, in fact, in a confusion of those allegations which are inherently false, with those allegations which, in the opinion of law enforcement officials, do not contain sufficient evidence to warrant prosecution.

In relation to all categories of crime, all detectives and all law enforcement agencies must make a distinction between those offences capable of proof in court and those with insufficient evidence. Using a variety of factors including corroboration, the identification of the offender and the demeanour and behaviour of the victim, the investigator has to exercise professional judgement to arrive at a decision in relation to each crime. On the basis of this judgement, police will decide with what vigour to pursue an allegation, and, if there is a suspect, whether or not to start proceedings. The exercise of this kind of discretion has a number of important implications. It allows police to husband the scarce resources of investigative units and it protects victims from the humiliation of a trial in which the defendant is likely to be acquitted. Difficult as the two matters are to reconcile, police also have a duty to protect suspects from the humiliation of court appearances which cannot be justified on the grounds of the weight of prosecution evidence.

This kind of distinction also has to be made by rape investigators. Rape investigators, however, face a kind of crime to which there are commonly no witnesses; from which there may be little forensic evidence; and about which there are widely held beliefs which may, as noted above, adversely affect the chances of a successful prosecution. Provided that the discretion as to how far to pursue an allegation is exercised on the grounds of evidence and the probability of conviction, and not, for instance, on some unreliable myth about rape or the failure of a victim to comply with an investigative stereotype,[1] then this is an essential area of judgement to be left to the professional investigator.

Discretion about whether or not to pursue allegations is more often exercised in cases of sexual assault than in other cases. This is rightly so, because the investigation of rape and other sexual offences is made more difficult by an additional problem. Even where the difficulties of collecting adequate forensic evidence and identifying the unknown assailant have been overcome, there remains the issue of consent. For the modern investigator, this is the corollary of Lord Chief Justice Hale's often quoted dictum concerning rape:

> It is an accusation easily to be made and hard to be proved, and harder to be defended by the party accused, tho' never so innocent *(Pleas of the Crown,* Vol. I, 1784).

It is also an area of hard decision making for the detective. If the difficulties described above are more common in relation to sexual offence investigations, then it should be expected that more rapes will end up as undetected allegations than is the case with other crimes. As noted below, however, criminal statistics from different jurisdictions indicate that low detection rates in rape investigations are far from universal. The consideration of why this is so and of the substantial variation in apparent detection rates helps to define the difference between those jurisdictions which pursue the 'new' approach to the investigation of sexual offences and those which do not.

Rape is a very serious crime and normally police administrators do not willingly accept a large proportion of undetected serious

56 *The problems of sexual offence investigation*

crimes. A solution to that problem is to ensure that some of those allegations which are unprosecutable do not remain on file as allegations. From that solution emerges the fallacy that a high number of allegations of sexual assault are false. This assumption may create serious additional stress for victims and cause evidence and criminal intelligence to be lost. In effect, confusing the exercise of discretion in relation to prosecution with the assumption that a report of rape is false will alter the balance between undetected and detected rapes in official criminal statistics.

That such a policy has been pursued by the police in the United States in the past is suggested by the different use that individual United States police departments make of three of the categories of final disposition of rape allegations: 'inactive' (the equivalent of undetected in the United Kingdom), 'unfounded' and 'victim withdraws allegation'.

Observation during the course of this study indicates that the San Francisco Police Department actively pursues a policy of discouraging victims from withdrawing allegations and only classifies cases as unfounded where there is extremely strong evidence that the victim is lying. The police department is, therefore, prepared to keep a high proportion of inactive cases on its files. (The reasons for this policy are discussed below.) During the years 1980 to 1982, only 2.25 per cent of the 2,485 cases of serious sexual assault investigated were classified as unfounded. In 13.7 per cent of cases victims withdrew their allegations and 49.7 per cent of cases were classified as inactive (statistics supplied by San Francisco Police Department).

Table 5.3: Final disposition of rape allegations in the United States, 1977

	Kansas (N=328) %	New Orleans (N=237) %	Detroit (N=283) %	Phoenix (N=105) %	Seattle (N=300) %
Unfounded	6	14	1	4	3
Victim withdrew complaint	38	6	22	12	12
Inactive	17	29	53	54	52

The study *Forcible rape*, gives similar breakdowns for five other American cities in the year 1977. These are reproduced in Table 5.3. The proportion of cases withdrawn by the victim is usually not separately recorded by United States police departments, and was not available for either Los Angeles or Newark. However, both cities were able to supply figures for unfounded and inactive cases. In 1981 these were 1.5 per cent and 60 per cent in Los Angeles and 3.5 per cent and 43 per cent in Newark.

There is considerable variation within the different categories of disposal. There is, however, some similarity between the proportions in each category recorded by the police departments visited in this study, and the figures for Phoenix and Seattle. The figures for New Orleans and Kansas are quite different. It seemed likely that the explanation for these differences lay in departmental policy and the five police departments concerned were therefore asked to explain their policies. One department failed to reply and three were unable to supply current figures. However, Kansas City Police Department noted that:

> The Kansas City, Missouri, Police Department has very strict policies regarding the reporting of a crime, and this policy has not changed significantly in the last twenty-two years.

This statement is somewhat belied by the statistics of the final dispositions of rape allegations for 1982 which Kansas City also kindly supplied. The relevant figures are: unfounded, 6 per cent (6 per cent in 1977); complaint withdrawn by the victim, 12 per cent (38 per cent in 1977); and inactive, 43 per cent (17 per cent in 1977). While the actual number of rapes had increased from 328 to 396, the proportion of cases unfounded and withdrawn had changed from 44 per cent in 1977 to 18 per cent in 1982: the coincidence of the simultaneous reversal in the inactive category from 17 per cent in 1977 to 43 per cent in 1982 is remarkable. It is unlikely that there has been a sudden increase in the tenacity with which female complainants in Kansas pursue allegations of rape. It is more probable that there has been, albeit unofficially, a change in recording policy by the Kansas City Police Department. It is, of course, possible that there is some blurring between the various categories but the general trend is quite clear. Furthermore, there is considerable similarity between these 1982 figures and those for the same year for other police departments, like San Francisco, with definite policies on the matter.

The significance of the difference between the inactivation and the withdrawal of an allegation lies principally in the effect on the victim. As some American investigators have found in the aftermath of the Big Dan's Tavern case, there is no way to prevent some rape complainants from withdrawing an allegation through fear or embarrassment. There are, however, opportunities to encourage or discourage them from doing so. Observation for this study indicated that officers of the San Francisco Police Department make every effort to discourage victims from withdrawing complaints. Officers of the Sex Crimes Detail are aware of the feelings of guilt and shame associated with sexual assault and know that the victim will face her own internal pressures to stop co-operating with the prosecution. If the victim does withdraw, the conflict of these pressures is not resolved and her feelings of guilt may increase. If, following withdrawal of the prosecution, the victim becomes convinced that she has not been believed, or that officialdom believes that she was responsible for her own victimisation, the result must be further trauma and possible psychological damage. Even where officers are not wholly convinced by the allegations of the victim, the San Francisco Police Department does not encourage officers either to seek the withdrawal of allegations or necessarily to classify the complaint as unfounded. The attitude of both investigators and administrators is that in the majority of cases, classifying cases as unfounded or withdrawn is acting as judge and jury without the full facts. It is an unnecessary additional burden for the victim to bear. In order to protect the victim, therefore, doubtful cases are permitted to lie on file, often with little further investigation.

United States detectives also claim that in addition to its beneficial effects for the victim, this policy provides them with increased evidence against repeat offenders. Cases marked unfounded or withdrawn are difficult to re-open if a subsequent rape by the same assailant is prosecuted. Forensic evidence, of course, will not normally be examined or preserved for the purpose of identification in the case of allegations not under investigation.

The general policy of keeping cases inactive is followed in Newark and Los Angeles as well as in San Francisco. The final disposition statistics suggests that these policies are also current in Seattle and in Phoenix. On the basis of the limited data outlined above, it would appear that similar guidelines are now being followed in Kansas City.

The question as to whether the numbers of undetected sex offences are similarly managed in the United Kingdom remains largely conjectural. In Britain, allegations of rape for which police decide the evidence is insufficient to substantiate that a crime has been committed (not, it should be noted, insufficient to support a prosecution), or in relation to which the victim withdraws her allegations are, save in wholly exceptional circumstances, classified as 'no-crime'. Were Kansas to be in Britain, the 44 per cent of rape allegations classified there as unfounded or victim withdraws allegations would have been classified as no-crime.

The problem that faces researchers in the United Kingdom in relation to the classification no-crime, is that allegations so classified do not appear in criminal statistics, and no central record is maintained of them which reveals the nature of the original allegation. Except for the physical search of crime records, there is no easy method of discovering the proportion of allegations of sexual assault which are classified as no-crime. At the time of preparation of this study such figures were not available either for England and Wales or for Scotland. It therefore remains possible that there are very few such allegations; that very few victims withdraw their complaints; and that very few rapists escape eventual detection and conviction in this way.

There are, however, some indications that this is not the case and that the number of allegations classified as no-crime may be considerable. The first indication comes from Chambers and Millar. This study revealed that 22.4 per cent of allegations of serious sexual assault were being classified as no-crimes by two Scottish police forces (p. 10). Despite the controversy aroused by Chambers' and Millar's report, there is little in it to suggest marked differences in the approach taken by Scottish police from that observable in their counterparts south of the border. In addition, Chambers and Millar noted that 30 per cent of the cases sent by police to the procurator fiscal were subsequently not proceeded with. Some of these cases would have been classified as no-crime in England and Wales. It might well be, therefore, that a similar study in England and Wales would detect a proportion of offences marked no-crime in excess of 22 per cent.

The second factor which suggests there may be some need for concern in the United Kingdom is derived from a comparison of detection rates. As mentioned in Chapter 2, the comparison of crimes cleared up in England and Wales with crimes cleared in the United States is difficult. American crime statistics are classified under four sub-headings: cleared (usually by arrest); exceptionally

60 *The problems of sexual offence investigation*

cleared (including allegations withdrawn and not prosecuted by district attorneys); unfounded; and inactive. To arrive at a comparison with United Kingdom figures, exceptionally cleared and unfounded allegations must be removed from the total number of allegations before the proportion cleared is compared with those classified as inactive. This cannot always be done because the statistics available cannot be divided in this way. For instance, the overall clearance rate of 51 per cent quoted in Chapter 2 and drawn from Uniform Crime Reports for 1982, includes both those crimes cleared by arrest and those exceptionally cleared. This figure cannot be further subdivided.

It is, however, possible to arrive at figures for detected offences for the five cities described in Table 5.3 for 1977 and for the San Francisco Police Department for the years 1981-2 which can be compared with figures for England and Wales. The figures in Table 5.4 were derived by comparing the total number of cases cleared by arrest with the total left inactive. Cases classified as unfounded and exceptionally cleared were removed from the analysis.

Table 5.4: Detection rates for six United States police departments

Detroit	Phoenix	Seattle	New Orleans	Kansas	San Francisco
1977	1977	1977	1977	1977	1981–82
%	%	%	%	%	%
27	30	27	48	49	36

Together with Table 5.3, Table 5.4 indicates that the detection rate may well be an indicator of the policy pursued in relation to classifying allegations as withdrawn or unfounded (that is, no-crimes in the United Kingdom). There is a broad correlation between high detection rates and a high proportion of allegations classified as withdrawn and unfounded and between high detection rates and a low proportion of allegations classified as inactive. In other words, high detection rates seem to go hand in hand with police recording practices aimed at disposing of crimes in the interests of administrative convenience (that is, as unfounded or withdrawn) rather than in the interests of the victim (that is, as inactive). Although there is clearly a limit to how far this argument can be taken—low detection rates may also indicate poor police performance—it is generally supported by these figures and also by the case of San Francisco Police Department. The Department's

Sex Crimes Detail is an efficient, dedicated unit of skilled detectives which deliberately discourages complainants from withdrawing allegations, yet its clear-up rate of 36 per cent is lower than some others in the table.

The relevance of this argument to Britain is clear. If the same technique of removing no-crimes and no-proceedings is used on Chambers' and Millar's data then police in Glasgow and Edinburgh achieved a 61 per cent clear-up rate. The 1982 clear-up rate for England and Wales was 68 per cent (Home Office, 1983b). While this compares favourably with the clear-up rates for other serious crime, it is considerably higher than would be expected given the difficulties of rape investigation. It may well indicate that a number of the less readily detectable offences are being classified as no-crime rather than as undetected. Support for this possibility can be found in a number of studies of no-crime rates as a product of police decision making, most notably in the work of Bottomley and Coleman (1980).

The third indication that many rapes are no-crimed derives from the author's subjective observations. First, some police officers in the United Kingdom readily give the impression of believing that a large number of rape allegations are false (see Chambers and Millar, pp. 81-7). The confusion between the falsity of a complaint and its unsuitability for prosecution on grounds of insufficient evidence therefore seems to exist in the United Kingdom. Secondly, during observation of sex crimes investigation in the United States, it was apparent that a different emphasis existed in detective practice. Because they had received training in the nature of rape trauma and its connection with police handling of the victim, US detectives were most determined in their efforts to dissuade the victims from withdrawing allegations even in doubtful cases. This approach seems to be less common in the United Kingdom.

If these arguments are accepted then some action is necessary. First, however, it is important to point out that the incorrect classification of an allegation as no-crime does not imply police malpractice. Individual officers may merely be taking practical decisions on the basis of evidence available to them. As Bottomley and Coleman note in another context, there is:

> no clear evidence to suggest a purposeful manipulation of crime statistics by the police for political or other purposes in Britain (p. 152).

If, however, too many cases are being classified as no-crime then victims will be suffering unnecessary trauma and society will be losing opportunities to apprehend offenders. It may be, of course, that there are few cases so classified in the United Kingdom, but there is clearly a need either for action or for further research.

If action is taken to restrict the number of crimes classified as no-crime, then guidance will have to be given to investigators about the limits of the proper exercise of their discretion. Police authorities will have to be prepared to accept a higher proportion of undetected cases. That in itself may take some political courage. While the actual number of arrests for rape in Kansas City rose from 82 in 1977 to 106 in 1982, thus keeping in step with the rise in the number of allegations, the proportion cleared of all cases classified as rape fell from 49 per cent to 37 per cent. That, unfortunately, would be how a change in the clear-up rate would be reported in the United Kingdom. Whether any chief officer of police would be prepared to accept similar reductions in clear-up rates in the interests of victims and the possibility of apprehending more offenders remains an open question.

The defence of consent

The consent of the victim is a defence only to crimes involving assault or indecency: it is encountered most frequently in the latter. It poses considerable problems for investigators of sexual crime because it offers a complete defence to the charge. In rape and sexual offences, the defence of consent can be expected in the majority of cases in which the two parties to the rape either knew each other before the time of the offence, or spent some time in each other's company before its commission. These are cases in which the identity of the suspect is not in dispute and in which forensic, as opposed to medical, evidence is unlikely to assist the prosecution, because intercourse by the defendant is admitted.

The methods by which the issue of consent is raised by the defendant and the difficulties it causes for the prosecution are the same in the United States as in the United Kingdom and need not be considered here. In relation to the police investigation, however, there is a major difference in training and procedure between the two countries. Some American police departments train their detectives in a particular method of investigating rapes in which consent is likely to be the issue. In Newark, for instance, detectives are taught to separate this kind of case from other offences and to anticipate the defence strategy concerning the acquaintance of the two parties and the motives underlying the woman's allegations. Officers are encouraged to move the focus of their investigation from the rape itself to its surrounding circumstances and to divide those circumstances into five areas: initial contact; coercive efforts; intimidation; rape; and report. Attention is also given to the movements of the victim and offender before and after the rape, and the manner in which those movements may indicate coercion and intimidation. In addition, officers are given careful instruction as to the nature of consent. The sexual assault investigators interviewed as part of this study endeavoured to ensure that their working definition of consent was neither based on assumptions of sexual dominance or compliance nor more extreme than that which would be accepted in a court of law. Detectives concentrated not only on proving that the victim had not consented but on obtaining evidence about the suspect's behaviour to determine whether or not he had sought consent.

These two areas of training succeed in focusing the attention of both detective and victim upon the actions, criminal responsibility and possible culpability of the suspect. The detective is required to focus on corroboration of the victim's account by considering the dynamics of the social interaction involved. He has to look for, but is not absolutely required to obtain, that corroboration of the use of physical force or intimidation by the suspect, which is favoured by law but is so often unobtainable.

No such training appears to be available in the United Kingdom. Chambers and Millar found that some investigators in Scotland could have been more accurate in their assessment of the meaning of consent, both in terms of the legal standard of evidence and, more broadly, in terms of the development of human sexual relationships. Chambers and Millar refer to this preferred investigative standpoint as 'bipartisan' (p. 92). The introduction of this approach to the defence of consent would no doubt have similar effects in the United Kingdom as in the United States: a reduction in the number of cases classified as unfounded and an increase in victims' ability to appreciate and maintain their sense of dignity and control over self.

The issue of consent will continue to present great difficulties for detectives and subsequently for juries. The approach followed in the United States, however, can produce lines of enquiry and facets of evidence which can otherwise be missed and indicate new strategies for the interrogation of a suspect in rape cases. It conforms with an ideal of dignified treatment for the victim of sexual assault. Best practice in the United States shows what can be achieved in rape investigation by careful research and analysis.

Note

1. See Clark and Lewis, 1977, pp. 17ff. and Chambers and Miller, pp. 87–90.

6 THE AMERICAN APPROACH TO INVESTIGATION

Attitudinal change

The response of police in the United States to the problems of rape investigation described above has been shaped by pressure from the women's movement. Under that pressure the police reappraised their thinking in four areas: the nature of the crime; the status of the victim, her rights and her role in the process of investigation; the function of the police investigator in relation to other agencies of society; and the duty of police to reassure the public that police attitudes and training are adequate in the light of re-evaluation of these other areas. This reappraisal has resulted in an approach to rape and rape victims which can only be described as radically different from that commonly found in the United Kingdom. It is true that the police departments visited during this study are not representative of every other police department in the United States because they each maintained specialist sex investigation units with advanced techniques. It is quite apparent, however, that this type of unit and these types of techniques are representative of a major proportion of United States police departments (see Center for Women Policy Studies, 1974). It is clear that a change has occurred and is occurring, and that what has been termed the 'new approach' is spreading throughout the United States.

The primary change involved in the 'new approach' lies in how the crime of rape and the victims of rape are perceived. During fieldwork for this study, the quotation from Burgess and Holmstrom which prefaces this report was quoted frequently by police officers. Many of them were also aware of Groth's findings that rapists are fulfilling aggressive rather than sexual urges. Frequent contact with different rape victims seems to leave sex crimes investigators in no doubt that the primary response of victims to rape is fear: fear of injury, mutilation and death. This perception of the crime enables detectives investigating rape to remove, or at least decrease, the sexual aspect of the crime from their approach to the victim. At the same time, they are aware of the effects of sexual taboos on the responses of the victim and treat complainants in accordance with their knowledge of rape trauma syndrome. Sex crimes investigators appear to pride themselves upon taking a non-judgemental view of all aspects of the behaviour and history of the victim.

The crime is thus viewed in relation to the rights of the victim rather than the necessary and arbitrary demands of the investigative process. Although rather strident in tone, the approach of the booklet *Survivor* may perhaps be regarded as typical. The compilers of this booklet suggest that the rights of a victim in connection with law enforcement include: confidentiality; the display of sensitivity by law enforcement officials; the availability of officers of both sexes; the maintenance of contact from allegation to trial; and the provision of information concerning the disposition of the case. In short, although it is the increased efficiency of investigations which must represent the principal benefit to police administrators, the symbol of the new approach to rape investigation in the United States is the significance accorded by investigators to the rights of the victim.

Interview techniques

The main contact between detective and complainant in the investigation of rape is the interview, or series of interviews, in which the allegation is outlined. Not surprisingly, therefore, it is in relation to the interview with the victim that the procedures adopted by American police departments are most clearly differentiated from standard British practice.

First, officers have been made aware in training of the theory of crisis intervention and the suggestibility of victims of crisis. Officers understood that it was their task to decrease feelings of guilt and embarrassment. During victim interviews, emphasis was placed upon the blamelessness of the victim and a thorough explanation was given of the reasons for detailed questioning concerning sexual acts. Interviews with victims were typically introduced as follows:

> I am going to ask you a lot of questions about what has happened to you. Before we go any further, I want you to understand that I have been involved in the investigation of this sort of crime for some years. Nothing you can tell me will shock me. I want you to treat me like a doctor: unless we take the case to court, everything you tell me will remain confidential. I want you to feel that

nothing that has happened to you is your fault. Nothing I am going to ask you will be unnecessary, and I will explain the need for any question about which you are concerned.

Officers conduct interviews either alone or with a single colleague. Every effort is made to ensure that the same officer continues with the investigation of the case. In the two nationwide surveys *Forcible rape* and *Rape and its victims* (Center for Women Policy Studies), much attention was focused on the question of whether women officers should conduct rape investigations. The conclusion of both enquiries is perhaps best expressed in *Forcible rape*:

> The gender of the officer is not as important as the qualities he or she possesses. Both men and women can be motivated, sensitive and understanding. The majority of rape victims express no preference concerning the sex of the investigating officers (Vol. IV, p. 17).

Both surveys conclude by recommending that women officers be available if required. Although the units observed for this study did have mixed sex teams, specific requests for a female officer seemed to be very rare. It is particularly interesting to note that personnel at the San Francisco Sexual Trauma Services, and the Santa Monica Rape Treatment Center, believed that, for psychological good health, a sympathetic male provided the most appropriate investigator for a heterosexual female complainant. Child victims were, however, generally interviewed by female officers.

In view of current procedure in the United Kingdom it was also interesting to find that United States police departments did not make use of non-detective female officers to take statements. When asked to comment on this procedure, American investigators did not see the need for it and thought it would hinder the development of an effective relationship with the complainant. It was their opinion that the successful achievement of empathy with the victim enabled a male officer to ask any kind of intimate question without causing embarrassment.

Another dissimilarity was that the location of the interview and the wishes of the victim about it were seen as important, and American officers readily interviewed complainants in their own home. However, the most fundamental procedural difference between the United States and the United Kingdom arises out of the timing of the interview.

American police practice is normally to make every effort to reduce the amount of information required at the time of reporting. Police will record sufficient details to identify the assailant or to prevent the escape of an unknown attacker. The quantity and quality of information required is left to the discretion of the investigating officer. After a medical examination, the victim is then escorted or allowed to go home and rest. Action is taken to apprehend and if necessary interview the suspect, and the victim then returns refreshed by sleep to make a full statement. Police officers in the United States regard this as being only consistent with the human rights of the victim.

In the United Kingdom, on the other hand, delaying the main interview in a case of rape is not normal practice. While there has been no general survey of British police procedure and while, for instance, Metropolitan Police regulations discourage immediate interviewing in the case of young women and children, it is the author's own experience that detectives normally take a full statement from the victim of rape at the time of report. That observation is supported by the findings of Chambers and Millar, who, in relation to the 200 cases in their survey, noted only one in which the victim went home before the main interview took place (pp. 66ff).

Coupled with the unavoidable length of time that must be spent in the process of medical examination, a complete police interview carried out at the time of first report will result in victims remaining at police stations for long hours. This may not only be distressing to the victim, it may also be unhelpful to the investigation. The American experience is that the evidence in a statement obtained from a victim who has had the opportunity to rest is greater in detail and internally more consistent than would be the case if it were fully recorded at the time of reporting. American practice is consistent with those studies of crisis theory and of rape trauma syndrome which have found that among the immediate reactions displayed by victims of crisis are the suppression of detail and the blocking of memory. The victim is the primary source of evidence in an investigation of rape. Chambers and Millar note, for instance, that over half of suspects are detected through the victim's knowledge or description (pp. 58-9). Delay in the interview ensures that the formal statement represents the most complete and the most accurate account of the assault and prevents the recording of inaccuracies which may later be used by the defence to cast doubt on the testimony of the complainant. Apparently, police practice in the United States used to be similar to that described by Chambers and Millar for Scotland and which, it is suggested, remains common in the United Kingdom. While the timing of the interview must remain a matter of professional discretion, a general change to a delayed interview has been found to be of material assistance both to victims and to investigators.

Training

The attitudinal and procedural changes just described are clearly reflected in the training of American police personnel. All jurisdictions that were visited had made efforts, either formally or informally, to train officers to accept, understand and use these new procedures. The training curricula of the New Jersey State Police, the New York Police Department and the Los Angeles Police Department all contain formal lectures on the myths of rape, on rape trauma syndrome and on interview techniques. There exists a Sexual Assault Investigators' Association of California whose annual meetings include seminars on methods of increasing sensitivity to particular issues (sensitisation), on the stress that continuous work in this field can put on personnel (burn-out) and on new forensic techniques. Guest speakers on a whole range of these and other topics attend these meetings.

In Greater Los Angeles, the Rape Treatment Center has been instrumental in training all officers from the Santa Monica Police Department. For patrol officers, the Center concentrates on a short lecture on the immediate effects of sexual assault. The responding patrol officer is given guidelines on how to cope with the victim's needs and prevent further traumatisation by avoiding authoritarian or judgemental questioning. For detectives, the instruction involves the filmed interview of a rape victim revealing the impact of the crime upon her; group discussion of interviewing techniques; and a number of exercises using written scenarios which require individual officers to deal with specified incidents.

Instruction at the Los Angeles Police Department follows broadly similar lines. The San Francisco Sex Crimes Detail has had no formal training for some years because each officer serves a period of apprenticeship on this small unit. They are, however, in such close liaison with the Sexual Trauma Services that each officer regularly attends the Central Emergency Hospital and is kept well informed about the various developments in the field. Staff of the Sexual Trauma Services, however, do train recruits and patrol officers. This instruction follows much the same form as the Rape Treatment Center syllabus but includes a discussion on the myths and facts of sexual assault. The Sexual Trauma Services also produce a short guide to rape trauma syndrome which is used to lecture to police groups, medical personnel and social workers (see Appendix E).

The most advanced centre for the study of crime and law enforcement in the United States is probably the John Jay College of Criminal Justice, New York. The acknowledged expert in the field of sexual offences at this college is Professor O'Reilly. He and other academics and police officers hold occasional seminars for police officers at the college. In September 1982, for instance, Professor O'Reilly chaired a three-day course at the John Jay College, during the course of which lectures and discussions were held upon the following topics:

> Overview: Rape—the myths and the reality
> Crisis intervention with victims of forcible rape
> Interviewing techniques
> Profile of a rape situation
> Aiding the victim: services in the community
> Profile of the rapist and interrogation techniques
> Sexual deviations and perversions
> Sex-related homicide and auto-erotic death
> Duties of the responding officer
> Duties of the investigator
> Evidence gathering and crime scene processing
> Developing a pertinent rape prevention programme
> The child as sex crime victim

The scope of this seminar, which was held for officers who already had considerable experience in investigating sexual assault, serves to demonstrate how American training in this field has developed.

Liaison with non-police agencies

As a result of the interest taken in the topic of rape by women's groups in the United States and the emergence of rape crisis centres as medico-legal pressure groups, police have also had to adjust their perception of their own position in regard to the process of investigation. In some respects the investigation of the crime is now seen as part of the treatment of the victim and police appear to be eager to co-operate with other agencies assisting the complainant. The process by which both San Francisco and Los Angeles observed and accommodated the pressures from women's groups has already been described. This process appears to have been repeated in many other parts of the United States. Law enforcement has been able to relinquish sole responsibility for the victim and, by the use of co-operation rather than confrontation, proper demarcation has been established between the functions of police and other related agencies. Full co-operation has also enabled police to present a positive public image through the media. Most important of all, however, the police have learned methods and approaches from the other agencies, and as co-operation has flourished and hostility has faded, the lot of the rape victim has improved.

Publicity

As in the United Kingdom, police and police departments in the United States have often received a bad press. In the field of sexual assault much press interest was shown in the various shortcomings displayed by police departments in the early 1970s. Many police departments have learned by the experience and are now using sex crimes investigation as a good advertisement for their department, while continuing to use the media to assist in rape investigations.

This is a two-way process. The media are only prepared to assist if the police department shows full co-operation. All of the departments which were visited had offered this to the media and, because of public fascination with sexual crime, the media had seized upon the chance. The police departments in question had paraded the advanced training and sympathetic attitudes of the new units before the public gaze and these were fully recorded in the press.

The sex crimes units also use the press for other objectives: for public education, rape prevention and the encouragement of reporting. All units had prepared leaflets announcing the existence of a sex crimes investigation team, encouraging victims to report crimes to it and giving advice as to how to contact the team and what evidence to preserve. Sex crimes teams produce leaflets on rape prevention and awareness and the New York Police Department pamphlet, *Beware. . . be aware* (at Appendix F), is an example of a crime prevention leaflet aimed specifically at this offence. Officers of all units give lectures to schools, universities, hospitals and many other groups of women on rape prevention and the preservation of evidence in the event of an attack. By fully co-operating with the media, sex crimes investigators have been able to arrange for the contents of leaflets and lectures to be printed or broadcast word for word; and members have given interviews to press, radio and television. The telephone numbers of the rape squads in Newark and San Francisco are displayed on public transport and public buildings.

Publicity is also being used in the United States to encourage the report of every rape. The Newark Police Department leaflet, *Silence frees a rapist* (at Appendix G), is a particularly effective example of the official encouragement of rape reporting. In some jurisdictions, this has initially resulted in an increase in the incidence of reported rape. Police departments have accepted that this means that they will have more accurate information about the levels of crime within their area, thereby enabling them to offer an improved service to women and to improve the possibilities of detecting persistent offenders. This is far from the only benefit. Investigators have also found that increased publicity improves awareness of rape preventive measures and educates the public about the facts as opposed to the myths of rape. This last benefit is difficult to evaluate, but better public understanding of rape may result not only in victims receiving kinder treatment from their peers, but also more responsible treatment from the potential jurors among the public reached by the media.

7 RECOMMENDATIONS: POLICE IN THE UNITED KINGDOM — TOWARDS A NEW APPROACH

Despite many surface differences, the composition of their peoples, the balances of their legal systems and the common bonds of their culture and history mean that social developments in the United States are likely to be reflected subsequently in the United Kingdom. The incidence of rape in both countries has grown quickly in recent years. In the past decade rape has become one of the major political issues in law enforcement in the United States. If, as seems likely, the political influence of women increases in Britain, it would appear inevitable that interest in rape will grow and so will pressure for reform.

The United States government has invested millions of dollars in research into rape and in the development and monitoring of rape investigation programmes. Because of the similarity between the two nations, the volume of knowledge and understanding produced by research in the United States is likely to be of great significance for police in the United Kingdom. Law enforcement personnel in the United States base their activities upon two fundamental findings of recent research. The first is that there is no miracle cure. No startling developments have been made in rape prevention, the identification of assailants, detection techniques or forensic science. The inescapable conclusion is that detection rates will not dramatically improve as a result of any technical innovation. (In fact, as is argued in Chapter 5, the purely statistical clear-up rate is likely to drop as a result of improvements in police methods.) As a consequence of this, law enforcement efforts in the United States have become concentrated upon the victim. The rediscovery that the victim represents the best evidence available to the prosecution is the second and major result of research into rape in the United States. Police techniques in America are now designed to protect the victim from the psychological damage of the crime in order to fulfil the primary police function of protecting the citizen from the consequences of crime. These techniques also enable police to obtain the best possible evidence from the victim and to sustain her as a witness during the ensuing legal procedures.

Although it is principally a restatement of well-known values, this police strategy has been characterised as a 'new approach' because its effects on police, the victim and the public at large represent such a marked departure from previous standards. It must be admitted, however, that the results of the reform are difficult to quantify.

Such detection rates as can be calculated are entirely favourable to the United Kingdom. This report has argued that the high detection rate in Britain is likely to be, at least in part, an artefact of police recording practices. In addition, United States police officers face a crime rate ten to fifteen times as great as their colleagues in Britain. Although the sex crimes units which were visited as part of this study appeared to be highly motivated and particularly efficient, there is no statistical evidence that the improved police techniques they use help to detect a greater proportion of rapists than do police procedures in Britain. It is possible to argue that the increased crime intelligence and improved quality of evidence resulting from such reforms must be of assistance to police, but only a specifically designed study could test this. At present, the arguments for reform must be based on other grounds. First, the use of improved techniques ensures that the particular effects of this horrific crime upon the victim are minimised as far as possible. Secondly, because they publicise them so comprehensively, police departments which employ these methods enjoy the increased confidence of the population and the political pressure groups within their police area. The third argument in favour of reform is that the introduction of similar methods in the United Kingdom would be unlikely to involve any increase in expenditure, or any capital investment or new equipment. Finally, the time is now right: public disquiet about rape is more likely to increase than disappear.

The findings of this study indicate that improvements in police techniques and skill can be learned from the experience of police in the United States and can be taught to others. The changes recommended below have the merit of being practically expedient and ethically desirable. Taken together, they represent a 'new approach for police', which would appear to offer substantial benefits both to future victims of rape and their investigators.

Medical procedures

It is clearly impossible for police surgeons in Britain to undertake the full range of functions carried out by medical personnel in the United States. Leaving aside consideration of the medical benefits to victims of the American approach, it is vital from a police point of view that the potential witness should be as fully reassured as possible by her medical examination. It is therefore recommended that all police surgeons deal fully with victims' fears of pregnancy and sexually transmitted diseases. It seems appropriate that the leaflet prepared by the Association of Police Surgeons of Great Britain (see Appendix D) should be available for use in all force areas. The question of whether the responsibility for conducting sexual offence investigations should be equally allotted to all police surgeons, or restricted to a limited number of them, lies outside the scope of this study, but ought to be examined. It seems important that attendance at specialised training sessions on sexual assault should be compulsory for those police surgeons who are to carry out examinations in such cases. It may be also considered appropriate that such training should now include some discussion of rape trauma syndrome. It is to be hoped that the diagram for the recording of trauma by police surgeons which is currently being considered by the Association of Chief Police Officers is accepted. Furthermore, it is to be hoped that consideration can now be given to the introduction of a standard comprehensive reporting form, including diagrams, for the use of all medical personnel in all cases of sexual assault.

Specialist units or specially trained officers?

Throughout this report it has been suggested that rape is a crime which presents unique difficulties to the investigator. Dealing with rape requires close co-operation between investigators and other departments inside the police service and between investigators and external agencies. Rape demands an understanding of the particular suffering caused to its victims and it should be investigated by officers capable of displaying appropriate sensitivity. Without exception, every person interviewed in the United States during the course of this study was quite certain that the specialist unit was the ideal model for the investigation of sexual crime. Sex crimes investigators displayed considerable pride in the expertise with which they dealt with offences, particularly in relation to victims.

All these considerations may be thought to represent cogent arguments in favour of the establishment of such units in the United Kingdom. However, there are three arguments against using this model in Britain. First, squads specialising in the investigation of particular crimes are the standard pattern of American detective bureaux, and a rape squad is an entirely natural development. The establishment of such a unit would not fit well with common practice in the United Kingdom where rape and homicide have traditionally been investigated by generalist local detectives and squads are more usually associated with the investigation of travelling or organised criminals. Secondly, United States detectives rely heavily on patrol officers to seal scenes, deal initially with victims and collect forensic evidence. This is not accepted practice in the United Kingdom. These procedures allow American detectives generally to investigate rape during office hours. Table 7.1 draws on the survey *Forcible rape* (Vol. I, p. 20) and Chambers' and Millar's study (pp. 17-18), to show the time of day and days of the week when rapes are reported.

Table 7.1: Time of day and days of the week when rapes are reported, United States and Scotland

Time of day	United States %	Scotland %
8 am–2 pm	9.25	6.6
2 pm–8 pm	15.47	17.3
8 pm–2 am	51.25	58.2
2 am–8 am	23.97	16.8
Day of week		
Weekend	55.05[a]	51.6[b]
Weekdays	47.95	48.4

Notes:
a. Friday evenings to Sunday evenings.
b. Friday, Saturday and Sunday inclusive.

According to these statistics, over 50 per cent of rapes occur at the weekend and nearly 75 per cent at night. Any single, specialised unit in any police force in Britain would have to deploy adequate numbers of detectives to cover those times.

Thirdly, the incidence of rape in the United States has reached levels at which police departments covering even small geographic areas receive sufficient complaints of rape to justify the maintenance of a dedicated unit. The survey *Forcible rape* suggested that each investigator should be responsible for 50 cases per year (Vol. IV, p. 14) and this would not seem an unreasonable figure. It has already been suggested that recorded rapes in the United Kingdom may not adequately represent the number of rapes reported to police. Even if, for the purposes of argument, the 285 offences of rape recorded in the Metropolitan Police District in 1982 represented as little as one half of the number of cases reported, on the basis of 50 cases per year per officer, no more than 20 officers would be needed to cover the whole of the Metropolitan Police District. And even if as a result of increased public confidence in police treatment the number of reported rapes rose, it seems unlikely that the number of investigators needed would have to be increased to more than 30. It would be impossible for 30 officers to cover the 780 square miles of the Metropolitan Police District; nor could they provide an adequate service at night or weekends. It is unlikely that this situation would be greatly different in other police areas. Therefore, although Chambers and Millar call for the establishment of special units, manpower logistics appear to make them entirely inappropriate to Britain.

The question remains, should all detectives be equally responsible for sexual investigation and trained for it, or should certain detectives, while remaining deployed on normal duties, be specially selected and trained to deal with sexual crime wherever it may occur? It would be necessary for each police force to consider the balance between the expertise that would result from special training and increased experience, and the availability of that expertise when need arises; but it should be borne in mind that all the arguments rehearsed above in favour of specialisation in sex crimes investigation could be met by the introduction of specially selected, but geographically dispersed sex investigators.

Metropolitan Police General Orders already state that offences of rape 'will be investigated by an experienced CID officer, if possible a Detective Inspector'. The policy of the West Midlands Police is similar. Those who are planning new training courses for the Metropolitan Police are already considering restricting instruction on the investigation of rape to officers on the senior or advanced CID courses. Such a policy could be formalised across the United Kingdom: the management of rape investigations could be officially excluded from the responsibilities of junior detectives.

Experienced CID officers could then be nominated as sexual offence investigators and given specialised training courses. The question of training is considered below but in the light of these considerations, it is recommended that certain detective sergeants, detective inspectors and detective chief inspectors are selected and trained for duty as sexual offence investigators. They should be given responsibility for the investigation of all sexual offences within a given geographical area while remaining deployed on general CID duties with a *pro rata* reduction in workload. This method of deployment would have the striking advantage of preventing officers from being constantly involved in the investigation of offences relating to indecency, which has resulted in some United States police officers becoming emotionally exhausted, or 'burnt-out'.

This recommendation for the special selection of officers for sexual offence investigation is being considered by the working party set up to examine the Metropolitan Police procedures in relation to the investigation of rape and kindred sexual offences.

Personnel

While some victims of rape prefer to speak to a woman, some would rather speak to a male detective. It is therefore important that investigators of either sex are available. With the exception of the investigation of offences against children, experience in the United States has shown that the gender of the investigator is less important than his or her sensitivity and expertise. Selection for employment on the investigation of such offences should, therefore, clearly be based not upon gender but upon specific personality characteristics and behavioural style.

Three further considerations are of importance. First, in a profession currently still numerically dominated and largely commanded by men, it is vital that sexual assault is not seen as 'women's work', with all the pejorative overtones which that could be seen to imply. Secondly, there are not enough women police officers and certainly not enough experienced women CID officers to provide staff for sexual investigation without withdrawing them from all other types of investigation. In the Metropolitan Police, for instance, women comprised less than 15 per cent of force strength in September 1983 and, with 172 officers, less than 5 per cent of detective strength. Thirdly, it must be remembered that the investigator must be capable of empathy not only with the victim but with the suspect. In the same way as an all-male team might be inappropriate for every victim, an all-female team might encounter some difficulties with different kinds of male suspects. It is therefore important that women officers are available and it is certainly true that women officers who formerly served in specialist policewomen's departments still maintain considerable expertise in this field. Nevertheless, despite the strongly held opinions of many women's groups, it cannot be recommended that officers employed upon the investigation of sexual offences should exclusively, or even mainly, be female.

Police interview procedure

The interview with the victim is the centre of any rape investigation. Throughout this report it has been emphasised that the experience of police in the United States is that improved techniques at this interview, based upon a recognition of the rights of the victim, increase the quantity and quality of evidence obtained from her. It is essential that the interview be conducted in a sympathetic and non-judgemental manner; that the interviewer understands the nature of rape trauma, and is aware of the inconsistent and inaccurate memory recall of people in crisis. Officers can be trained to approach the interview in this way.

Three procedural changes are necessary, however, if the best possible evidence is to be obtained. First, it has been mentioned that the practice of using non-detective women officers to take statements is not common in the United States. American sex crimes investigators considered that the interviewer should be tactful enough to be able to elicit all necessary details from the victim and that for a third party to take a statement would be both inefficient and detrimental to the relationship between the victim and the interviewer. The victim should have the right to choose to be interviewed by an officer of either sex. If the officer is a male, the presence of a woman officer could be considered if it is felt that the victim would prefer this arrangement. However, it is recommended that whatever the sex of the investigator, he or she should conduct the interview and take the statement.

Secondly, there is no adequate reason to require a victim to make an immediate and lengthy statement. It is this practice, perhaps more than any other, which has been most heavily criticised by women's groups. After a medical examination and an interview of sufficient length to establish that an offence has occurred, and the identity, whereabouts or description of the suspect, the victim should be allowed to leave the police station and rest. There is nothing to prevent the arrest, detention and even interview of an alleged suspect while the victim is recovering from her ordeal. After rest and appropriate medical treatment, she will be better fitted to make a comprehensive and cogent statement. The timing of interviews must remain a matter of professional judgement because the circumstances of cases will vary. However, it is recommended that the practice of taking lengthy statements immediately after the crime be generally abandoned.

The third reform concerns policies about classifying rapes as no-crime and the withdrawal of allegations by victims. Although it is not official policy in any force to encourage the classification of allegations as to no-crimes nor to encourage the withdrawal of allegations by victims, there are good grounds from which to infer that a proportion of allegations made in Britain are being so classified and that this proportion is larger than it need be. While police must and will continue to exercise judgement as to which allegations will be pursued and which, for a variety of reasons, will not be investigated, it is clear that the use of a no-crime classification in inappropriate cases reduces police effectiveness. Where no-criming results from the victim withdrawing her allegation, the reinforcement of guilt may significantly increase the damage caused to her by the crime.

It is obviously more convenient both for the detectives and their supervisors for cases of rape to be terminated either by arrest or by classifying the crime as no-crime. The loss of evidence and the effect on the victim of such an unofficial policy, however, must outweigh any administrative convenience. Police administrators must ensure that clear directions are given that allegations should only be classified as no-crime in exceptional circumstances, and that every effort should be made by police to discourage victims from withdrawing allegations. The consequences of this change of policy will include a fall in the official clear-up rate for rape offences and an increase in the number of offences which are investigated less fully than might be possible. These two changes, which will be anathema to supervisory detectives, will be outweighed by improvements in the treatment received by victims and by improvements in the quality of evidence in individual cases and of crime intelligence in general. It is important that the rationale for these changes is carefully and comprehensively explained to police officers if their efficiency and morale is not to suffer as a result of adverse changes in the ostensible clear-up rate.

The importance of reform of police procedures for interviewing victims of sexual crime is revealed by Chambers' and Millar's study. They note that of those women who found any part of the investigation stressful, a large proportion were concerned about the interview: 47.8 per cent of these women felt that police interviewing practices were particularly stressful. A further 25 per cent were more generally concerned about police lack of consideration for their situation (p. 126). It would appear that training needs are beginning to emerge.

Training

In the United States, rape trauma syndrome, the theory of crisis intervention and the need for special sensitivity and empathy in the interviewing of rape victims are all taught to detectives, along with information about the collection and significance of forensic evidence and the defence of consent. The situation in the United Kingdom is that all police training includes lectures on the law of sexual offences. On initial detective courses some limited instruction is given on interview techniques, which may or may not include interviews with alleged rape victims. Detectives also receive adequate instruction in forensic science. Crisis intervention is a technique which is currently being evaluated in some training establishments (in the Metropolitan Police, for instance, it is being considered as part of the policing skills programme presently being introduced into the recruit syllabus). The provision of training on the effects of rape upon the victim, however, seems to be at the discretion of individual instructors. One result of this study is that the subject of rape trauma is being introduced into detective training courses in the Metropolitan Police.

It would be a relatively simple matter to create from these different efforts a unified body of training for all forces in the United Kingdom. Instruction on the effects of rape on its victims and the unique difficulties of rape investigation could be introduced at the four levels of police training with considerable effect.

Recruit training

Time is always allocated in police recruit syllabuses to instruction on the law of sexual offences. It would be possible to introduce a short period of instruction (perhaps using a brief video film) on the effects of rape upon the victim and the effects of police behaviour, both at the scene and at the police station, on her perception of her situation. Should the concept of crisis intervention be introduced into all British police training, as it is now being introduced into the Los Angeles Police Academy, then the treatment of rape victims by beat officers ought to be a topic of considerable importance.

Initial detective training

Time is allocated on Home Office approved initial detective courses for lectures on the law of sexual offences. Further time is given over to lectures on medical and forensic evidence in rape, and on interview techniques. Even if the investigation of rape were to be restricted to experienced detectives, it may well be a junior night-duty detective who has first contact with the victim. For this reason and particularly if rape investigation is not to be restricted to nominated officers, instruction should be given on initial CID courses on the effects of rape in general, of rape trauma in particular, their relationship to police treatment and on the approach to rape interviews. The police approach to rape and kindred sexual offences should be presented as a unified package and different methods of instruction including outside expert speakers, visual aids and group discussion should be employed as appropriate. Any change in police procedures in relation to the reporting and classification of rape allegations should be made clear.

Advanced detective training

Refresher courses for detective sergeants and advanced and forensic training for detective inspectors is already part of CID instruction. If officers are to be specially nominated as sexual offence investigators, it needs to be decided whether they should be trained on special short courses or as part of their advanced training. It may be necessary initially to hold a number of short courses and later to incorporate them into existing courses. In either case, advanced detective training should follow the same lines as initial training but cover topics in greater depth. It would also be possible to include special information about the behavioural patterns of rapists and give particular instruction about the investigation of the consent defence to rape. In the smaller groups available at advanced levels, it would certainly be possible to use different instructional techniques including role-playing, seminar and discussion groups.

Higher police training

Three areas could be covered in higher police training at the Police Staff College and at other training centres. Officers attending these courses should be informed of current thinking in relation to the whole area of sexual investigation. Instruction should be given about the management of sexual investigators, with particular emphasis on the part senior officers can play in relieving the pressure on subordinates to terminate cases either in prosecution or by classifying them as no-crimes. The appropriate selection procedures for officers employed on sexual investigation should be discussed, as should their rotation and redeployment in order to avoid 'burn-out'.

None of these changes should unduly increase the burden upon training institutions. Staff could be diverted from the courses on the investigation of sexual offences which are currently held for women police officers, which could be reduced in number. The emphasis of these existing courses could be changed from the taking of statements to the collection and preservation of evidence, particularly during the medical examination of victims of sexual assault.

Police policy on liaison and publicity

Liaison with non-police bodies

The initial reaction of United States police departments to the establishment of rape crisis centres was incredulity and hostility. By 1978, however, 65 per cent of police departments were aware of such a facility within their area and almost all investigators believed that such centres were of value (see Table 3.3 above).

In the United Kingdom, the establishment of rape crisis centres has been similarly controversial. Although some police forces enjoy a reasonable relationship with rape crisis centres in their police areas (see Table 3.4 above), there is still some suspicion and antipathy on the part of both police and centre staff. Of the two 24-hour centres, Birmingham has established a working relationship with the West Midlands Police but, for a variety of reasons, the London Rape Crisis Centre and the Metropolitan Police have been unable to achieve similar co-operation.

After initial non co-operation, police departments in the United States determined upon and were partly forced towards a policy of consultation with local rape crisis centres. They listened to the demands made upon them and made certain reforms. Publicising these reforms has won over a majority of concerned women to the view that police are dealing adequately with the crime. As the process of co-operation continued, the lot of the rape victim improved and strident criticism of the police over this issue became both less common and overtly less well founded.

Present developments in policing in Britain are in the direction of increased co-operation between police and those outside agencies concerned with the criminal process.[1] It is likely that these developments will lead to pressure for co-operation in the assistance offered to victims of rape. For the sake of the victims, it is vital that full co-operation is established between police and groups specifically concerned with rape victim support.

Experience in the United States suggests that the establishment of rape crisis centres leads to greater co-operation. This may also occur in the United Kingdom, with rape crisis centres appearing in increasing numbers and the London Rape Crisis Centre and the Metropolitan Police establishing rapport and liaison. It is more likely, however, that shortage of finance, lack of appropriate training and continuing differences in philosophy between police and rape crisis centre personnel will inhibit, if not prevent, the future growth of the rape crisis centre movement and its relationship with police in the United Kingdom.

For these reasons, it seems likely that victim support schemes will become increasingly involved in the care of rape victims. The purpose of the victim support schemes is to help the victims of crime to overcome some of the consequences of victimisation. Each scheme has three elements, drawn from the local community: a network of volunteers, a co-ordinator and a management committee. The names of the victims of particular crimes are passed by local police to the co-ordinator, who arranges for suitable members of the scheme to make contact with them. Some members of each management committee and many other ordinary members of the schemes have professional, medical, paramedical or social work qualifications.

In the early days of the victim support schemes, the victims of sexual assault were excluded from the ambit of their work because of the complexity of the issues involved. As their confidence has grown, however, many schemes have begun to move into the difficult fields both of sexual offences and of bereavement as a result of homicide. By October 1983, 62 of the 165 schemes registered with the National Association of Victims Support Schemes had either dealt with victims of sexual assault or had agreed a referral policy with the police.[2] A short training programme to equip volunteers to deal with sexual offence victims is currently under consideration by the Metropolitan Police and the National Association of Victims Support Schemes.

A network of volunteers of different backgrounds and abilities is unlikely to be as skilled in assisting victims to overcome the unique symptoms of sexual violation as would be professional counsellors dedicated to victims of this group of crimes. Nor will victim support schemes reach those many women who do not report rape and other sexual offences to police. If it is doubtful whether professionally run rape crisis centres will be widely established in the United Kingdom, then police referrals to local victim support schemes are likely to be the most effective compromise available. Where special crisis centres do appear, future co-operation with police may be achieved through liaison between these centres and victim support schemes. Whatever happens, the existence of the volunteers of the victim support schemes can only benefit the victims of sexual assault.

Publicity

Police in the United Kingdom should follow the example of the United States in relation to publicity: police forces should actively seek media coverage to publicise the attempt to improve police techniques in the investigation of rape and the treatment of rape victims. Emphasis should be placed on changes in procedures, training and co-operation with outside agencies. The media should be used to educate the public about the facts of sexual assault and the appropriate methods of rape prevention.

There is no doubt that the media will be eager to deal with the topics of rape and sexual crime: given full co-operation by the police, they will give wide coverage to a change in police attitudes.

Although care will have to be exercised to ensure that the media reflect these important changes without over-emphasising the more sensational aspects of the police treatment of the crime, chief officers of police in the United Kingdom will undoubtedly find, as their colleagues have done in the United States, thah public knowledge of improvements in sexual offence investigation is excellent publicity.

Notes

1. It is, for instance, the stated policy of the present Commissioner of Police of the Metropolis to pursue a multi-agency approach to crime prevention.
2. Figures supplied by the National Association of Victims Support Schemes, October 1983.

8 CONCLUSION

The purpose of this study was twofold: to make recommendations for the reform of British police procedures in relation to the investigation of rape, and to review the impact of a decade of change on the American approach to the crime. In examining developments in the United States and selecting those elements of a changed approach which seem most appropriate to the United Kingdom, I have set out to consider which reforms have been successful in ameliorating the trauma of victims and reassuring the American public of increased police effectiveness. Despite some of the failures and perhaps, from a British perspective, some of the hyperbole involved, American reforms must be regarded as a considerable success. The view from the other side of the Atlantic suggests that every effort should be made to hold the advances gained in the United States and to prevent other political pressures from once again relegating sexual assault investigation to a low priority.

For the United Kingdom the conclusion is very different. Urgent reform must be carried through as soon as possible, and much of the responsibility for that reform must fall on the police service. The responsibility for adequate and appropriate treatment of victims of sexual assault is not, however, that of the police alone. Other institutions and individuals also have effects upon and responsibilities towards victims. It is therefore not surprising that in addition to criticisms of police activity, research has indicated inadequacies in both the medical and judicial procedures that adversely affect the victims of sexual crime (Shapland; Holmstrom and Burgess). On a wider front, the treatment of the topic of sexual assault by the media has rarely been anything other than prurient and meretricious.

All research seems to indicate that it is the victim's early contacts with official institutions that are likely to have the most effect on her future well-being. In the United States, police investigators have the opportunity to form part of a whole network of agencies designed to support and protect the victim. In the United Kingdom, similar agencies are few and far between. Where they exist, either as rape crisis centres or as victim support schemes, they are at a relatively early stage of development. The health and social services are too short of funds and too committed to other urgent needs to be

88 Conclusion

able satisfactorily to alleviate the problems of victims of sexual assault. Whatever may happen in the future, police in the United Kingdom bear at present the main responsibility for dealing initially with rape victims. As a result, criticism about their performance cannot be deflected elsewhere, but, by the same token, responsibility for their present achievements and for any future improvements must be theirs alone.

It is not and it cannot be the task of police to assume the caring and counselling role provided by supportive agencies in the United States. It is for police in the United Kingdom to take every possible action to encourage the development of such agencies. In their absence, however, it is the duty of police unilaterally to improve their methods of investigation so as to offer the maximum assistance to rape victims within the boundaries of police responsibility. The police must also recognise and use the fact that rape is a major public issue and will consequently always be a matter of media concern. Having taken all necessary steps to improve investigative techniques and their own treatment of victims of sexual assault, police must then publicise their actions: in this particular field, reforms must not only occur but be seen to occur.

The experience of police in the United States has been that the most effective development in the investigation of rape is for detectives to treat rape victims in accordance with a knowledge of the particular effects of rape upon its victim, commonly termed rape trauma syndrome. This treatment has been found to enhance the quality of evidence and to reduce the suffering of the victim. At the same time it has resulted in a major improvement in police image and public relations. Police in the United Kingdom should, therefore, give urgent consideration to adopting such of the reforms outlined above as seem appropriate.

The experience of police departments in the United States should also be considered in relation to liaison with non-police agencies which provide support for victims. Full co-operation in this field, however, still lies in the future. At present, it is to police officers that many rape victims turn at the moment of their greatest distress. This is a grave responsibility. I believe that it can most properly be discharged by the creation and maintenance of a whole approach, a 'new approach', to the investigation of rape.

This study has been written in the hope that a consideration of this approach will enable the police service to treat the victim of rape with enhanced expertise, arising from a more complete understanding of the actual meaning of rape for each and every one of its victims.

Appendix A:
EXTRACT FROM *SURVIVOR.* BOOKLET PREPARED BY LOS ANGELES COMMISSION ON ASSAULTS AGAINST WOMEN

What are my rights?

Many survivors of violent crimes, and especially survivors of sexual assaults, experience emotional shock. At this time it is important for you to know that victims can become survivors. Part of this process is making every attempt you can to take control of your life again and being certain that you are receiving the care, information and rights to which you are entitled. By exercising your rights you are, in effect, taking charge again.

As a survivor:

YOU HAVE THE RIGHT to determine whether or not you want to report the sexual assault to law enforcement.

YOU HAVE THE RIGHT to request to be interviewed by a female officer if you decide to make a report. This may result in extremely lengthy delays in the reporting procedure.

YOU HAVE THE RIGHT to report but not proceed with prosecution.

YOU HAVE THE RIGHT to withdraw your testimony against the attacker at any time.

YOU HAVE THE RIGHT to reasonable protection by the law. In some cases you may be entitled to request any one or more of the following:
- escort to accompany you to and from court;
- additional patrol from the police car(s) assigned to your area;
- restraining order(s);
- under severe circumstances — relocation.

YOU HAVE THE RIGHT to be treated in a considerate and sensitive manner by law enforcement and prosecution personnel.

YOU HAVE THE RIGHT to sue a person or company for negligence if you were sexually assaulted in a place having unsafe conditions (apartment building or parking lot, for example).

YOU HAVE THE RIGHT to contact and be contacted (where and when you wish) by law enforcement and the District Attorney's Office.

YOU HAVE THE RIGHT to obtain copies of police reports regarding the sexual assault.

YOU HAVE THE RIGHT not to be exposed to prejudice because of your race, age, class, lifestyle, or occupation.

YOU HAVE THE RIGHT to be considered a rape survivor regardless of the relationship of the assailant to you (i.e. spouse, acquaintance, relative, etc.).

As a patient:

YOU HAVE THE RIGHT to gentleness and sensitivity during your medical examination.

YOU HAVE THE RIGHT to call your personal physician to attend you.

YOU HAVE THE RIGHT to refuse the collection of medical evidence, even though you may request venereal disease and pregnancy tests.

YOU HAVE THE RIGHT to privacy during the collection of medical evidence. Even though you may be a minor, you have the right to have the examination without a parent or guardian present.

YOU HAVE THE RIGHT to request that law enforcement officers leave the examining room.

YOU HAVE THE RIGHT to request that a friend, family member, or rape crisis counselor accompany you in the examination room.

YOU HAVE THE RIGHT to have each procedure explained in detail before it is done.

You have the right to survive.

YOU HAVE THE RIGHT to an explanation of the reason for every test, form, and procedure.

YOU HAVE THE RIGHT to copies of medical reports (by law as of January 1, 1983).

YOU HAVE THE RIGHT to make application for reimbursement through Victims of Violent Crimes Compensation for certain medical expenses. You also have the right to copies of documents or correspondence relating thereto. You are entitled to help in filling out these forms.

YOU HAVE THE RIGHT to strict confidentiality.

YOU HAVE THE RIGHT to have common reactions to the rape, such as sleeplessness, nightmares, anxiety, fear, etc., and *not* have these reactions considered abnormal behavior.

As a witness:

YOU HAVE THE RIGHT to be asked only those questions that are relevant to a court case.

YOU HAVE THE RIGHT to attend all proceedings which are not closed to you as a witness or to the public.

YOU HAVE THE RIGHT to a translator in court if you do not speak English.

YOU HAVE THE RIGHT to any court records which are public.

YOU HAVE THE RIGHT to have your own attorney present during the proceedings. If you are a minor, you have the right to testify in closed chambers or to have your parents excused from the courtroom during your testimony.

YOU HAVE THE RIGHT to sue the suspect in civil proceedings.

YOU HAVE THE RIGHT to make application for reimbursement through Victims of Violent Crimes Compensation for certain legal expenses. You also have the right to copies of documents or correspondence relating thereto.

YOU HAVE THE RIGHT to be informed of the parole date and release from jail if your assailant is found guilty and sent to prison.

YOU HAVE THE RIGHT to have someone with you (a friend, relative, advocate, etc.) at police and court proceedings such as line-up identifications or Superior Court.

YOU HAVE THE RIGHT not to be asked questions about prior sexual experience with anyone other than the defendant.

It is important to remember that you are entitled to and should demand to be kept informed of proceedings and reports, whether they are legal or medical. Also, be sure you know your rights and get all medical and psychological care that you may need.

Finally... **you have the right to survive**... which means that you have the right to request everything that you need in making the transition from victim to survivor.

Do I have to report this to the police?

Before your physical examination in the emergency room, you may have contacted law enforcement officers. If you did not, it is important for you to understand that most hospitals automatically contact law enforcement once you are there. *This does not mean that you are obligated to make a crime report.*

In some areas it is possible to make a "third-party report" to law enforcement. You or someone acting on your behalf can contact law enforcement by telephone. Your name (or the name of the person calling for you) does not have to be given. *You are the only one who can decide whether or not to make an initial crime report and how to report the crime.* In making that decision, keep the following facts in mind.

Advantages:

1. If you report the crime and the suspected rapist is caught and convicted, you may have protected others from falling victim to the rapist. Also, your reporting may help to substantiate another survivor's report.

2. You will be eligible for Victims of Violent Crimes Compensation provided by the State of California.

3. You can request assistance throughout the trial process from Victim Advocates and/or Crisis Counselors.

4. You are exercising your rights!

Disadvantages:

1. It may be difficult for you to repeat your story for what seems to be many times to law enforcement officers and in court.

2. The District Attorney has the right to decide whether or not to proceed with the case, although you are entitled to know why your case was not filed.

3. Less than one out of five cases goes to trial, and fewer result in conviction. This does not mean that your particular case will not be filed, but the statistics are discouraging. However, once filed and prosecuted there is an 84% conviction rate in L.A. County.

4. It may be emotionally difficult for you because you may relive the assault experience.

If you decide to report the assault, the first step is a crime report, which may take place before or after the physical examination in the emergency room. Within a few days after the initial report, special sexual assault investigators may call you into their office or come to you for a follow-up report.

You **must be truthful** in each statement you make in any law enforcement or judicial proceedings. Inaccurate or incorrect information may cause law enforcement to follow false leads. If you are not certain of something, be sure to say so. If you do not know something **exactly** describe as accurately as possible. Law enforcement officers will ask you questions regarding your name, address, phone number, and place of business. If you are unemployed, say so. Do not worry about your unemployment or resident status. The officers are not there to judge you. They are there to obtain information about the crime: the date and the time of the occurrence, location, description of the suspect, etc. Law enforcement officers will also ask about your activities before and after the assault.

Law enforcement officers should not ask you questions about your emotional or physical reaction at the time of the assault. (They should not ask, "Did you enjoy it?," Climax?," etc.) In some cases, law enforcement officers may ask

Appendix B:
CITIES HAVING RAPE CRISIS CENTRES IN THE UNITED KINGDOM, NOVEMBER 1983

London (24 Hours)
Birmingham (24 Hours)
Bradford
Brighton
Bristol
Cambridge
Canterbury
Cleveland
Coventry
Leamington
Leeds
Leicester
Liverpool
Manchester
Norwich
Nottingham
Oxford
Portsmouth
Plymouth
Reading
Sheffield
Tyneside
Aberdeen
Edinburgh
Glasgow
Belfast

Appendix C:
INFORMATION LEAFLET FOR VICTIMS TREATED BY SEXUAL TRAUMA SERVICES, SAN FRANCISCO

YOU HAVE HAD TESTS FOR THE FOLLOWING:

_____legal evidence
_____culture for gonorrhea
_____blood test for syphilis
_____blood test for existing pregnancy
_____other _____

THE FOLLOWING ITEMS WERE DISCUSSED WITH YOU:

_____care of your injuries_____
_____common feelings after sexual assault
_____risk of pregnancy. Judging from your medical history, pregnancy is:
   —highly unlikely   —unlikely   —possible.
_____possible venereal diseases and the spread of possible VD to partner.

YOU HAVE RECEIVED THE FOLLOWING TREATMENT, PRESCRIPTIONS OR ADVICE:

_____for injuries _____
    ____Tetanus Toxoid
_____for venereal disease prevention
    ____Ampicillin 3.5G: Benemid 1.0G
    ____Tetracycline 500 mg—4 times daily for 5 days
    ____Other_____
_____for pregnancy prevention—options discussed:
    ____wait for menstrual period   ____DES—"morning after" pill
    ____abortion   ____other _____

IT IS ADVISABLE TO RECEIVE THE FOLLOWING FOR THE SAKE OF YOUR OWN HEALTH:

_____in one week: a gonorrhea culture (GC)
_____in eight weeks: a blood test for syphilis (VDRL)
_____if your next menstrual period has not occurred within six weeks, have a pregnancy test done.

PLEASE CONTACT SEXUAL TRAUMA SERVICES REGARDING FOLLOW-UP APPOINTMENTS OR REFERRALS AS NECESSARY.

_____	_____ M.D.	_____ R.N.
Counselor	Physician	Nurse

Appendix D:
INFORMATION LEAFLET FOR VICTIMS. ASSOCIATION OF POLICE SURGEONS OF GREAT BRITAIN

Who is a Police Surgeon?
A police surgeon is not a policeman but a local family doctor who:
- has special experience in examining those who have been physically assaulted;
- will arrange for you to receive any necessary treatment;
- assists the police in their investigations.

What will the Police Surgeon do?
The police surgeon will, but only with your permission (or the permission of your legal guardian):
- examine you as thoroughly as necessary and as quickly as feasible.
- be as considerate as possible knowing that you may have already suffered a hurtful and frightening ordeal;
- respect your feelings and wishes at all times.

What will the Police Surgeon expect of you?
The police surgeon hopes that you will:
- be truthful, however embarrassing or unpleasant your experience;
- understand that all the questions and special tests asked of you are essential for a proper examination;
- realise that only by assisting to the best of your ability have the police any chance of preventing another possible attack on someone else.

If you have been sexually assaulted:
Unfortunately the medical aspects of your case may not yet be over but rest assured that the police surgeon will advise you of any further measures which should be undertaken to prevent ill health.

In addition, you are especially advised to consult your doctor if you develop any of the following symptoms:
- pain, sores or discharge affecting the private parts;
- sore throat;
- a delayed or otherwise abnormal monthly period.

From:
Dr. ....
Police Surgeon,
....
....

Dear Doctor .... Date ....
At .... hours on the .... I examined
.... aged ....
of ....
....

I believe her/him to be a patient of yours and I have her/his consent to relay to you the following information,

Nature of alleged offence ....
....

Significant clinical findings ....
....

The following treatment was given ....
....

May I suggest the following further action?
    Pregnancy screening
    S.T.D. screening
    Psychotherapy
    Other

Yours sincerely,

From:
Dr. ....
Police Surgeon,
....
....

Dear Doctor .... Date ....
At .... hours on the .... I examined
.... aged ....
of ....
....

Nature of alleged offence ....
....

Significant clinical findings ....
....

In view of the high incidence of Sexually Transmitted Disease associated with sexual assault, I would be grateful if you would exclude or treat any possible infection in this case.

Yours sincerely,

Appendix E:
RAPE TRAUMA SYNDROME. A GUIDE. SEXUAL TRAUMA SERVICES, SAN FRANCISCO

INITIAL REACTIONS TO SEXUAL ASSAULT

FACTS:
1. Sexual assault represents a major life crisis.
2. The emotional trauma accompanying sexual assault is the result of forced violation.
3. The vast majority of sexual assault victims do not need long-term psychiatric counseling as a result of the assault.
4. An effective crisis intervention counselor can help the victim return to her/his pre-assault level of functioning in a relatively short period of time.
5. Any life crisis can serve as a catalyst for reassessment of a person's lifestyle and interpersonal relationships.
6. A person in crisis does not necessarily behave in a logical or sensible way—nor are they necessarily hysterical or incoherent.
7. Crisis can lead to minor life disruptions or major disfunctions.
8. Studies have indicated that responses to sexual assault follow a somewhat sequential pattern.

RAPE TRAUMA SYNDROME—from the work of Burgess and Holmstrom with modifications from the experience of STS staff

During the attack:

Disbelief—Sexual assault is something that happens to someone else.
Terror—Fear of being killed or mutilated. The physical threat is a perceived reality for almost all victims because violence is an integral part of the act.
Vulnerability—An encompassing sense of powerlessness.
Sexual assault is experienced primarily as a physical assault—penis is used as a weapon.

Acute phase—Time period: a few days to weeks

Characteristics:

A. Visibly upset (Expressed)	Tearful/sobbing
	Inappropriate laughter/smiling
	Hostile/angry
	Fearful
	Tense
	Restless
B. Hidden emotion (Controlled)	Appears calm
	Reluctant to talk
	Talks about assault as if it happened to someone else

96 *Appendix E*

C. Combination
(Expressed and Controlled)

Physical characteristics:

    Overall soreness
    Soreness in the area of the body that was the focus of the assault
    Sleep pattern disturbances
    Eating pattern disturbances
    Disassociation with the body
    Anxiety about pregnancy, VD

Areas of concern/fears

    Fear of not being believed
    Generalized anxiety/non-specific
    Fear of physical exam/pelvic exam as re-assault
    Relations of significant others
    Fear of retaliation
    Powerlessness

Needs:

    To be heard and understood
    To feel safe
    To be believed
    To know/feel that she/he handled the attack in the best way possible for her/him
    To be accepted
    To have her/his needs met—medical, legal, counseling
    To be provided with enough information to make individual choices about medical care, police intervention, informing significant others, and counseling
    To feel in control and regain personal power

It must be remembered that the primary *initial* reaction to sexual assault is that of fear—fear of injury, mutilation or death.

The symptoms known as Rape Trauma Syndrome are an acute stress reaction to the perception of being killed. Feelings in conjunction with the fear of dying range from: humiliation, degradation, guilt, shame, embarrassment to self-blame, anger, revenge.

THE FIRST WEEKS/THE MONTHS FOLLOWING AN ASSAULT

Adjustment phase—Time period: Weeks—months
The adjustment phase focuses on the attempt by the victim to return a feeling of normalcy to her/his lifestyle. This normalcy represents security, comfort and the feeling of being in control.

Characteristics: Disorganization

    Denial/suppression

Appendix E 97

    Sleep disturbances
    Startle reactions
    Feelings of isolation
    Feelings of humiliation/embarrassment
    Feelings of dependency
    Flashbacks/obsessive memories
    Intensification of ongoing problems
    Breakdown of previously successful defenses

Areas of concern/fears:

    How the sexual assault will affect her/his future
    Indoor/outdoor phobias
    Fear of being approached from behind
    Anxiety in regard to resuming sexual activity
    Fear of rejection by significant others
    Rejection by significant others
    Fear of the unknown
    Loss of a sense of security
    Pregnancy

Needs:

    A change in residence, phone number, employment setting
    To be able to ventilate about the assault and subsequent feelings as often as desired
    To be supported in expressing her/his feelings
    To be supported from significant others
    To regain a sense of control over her/his life
    To integrate a new view of her/his self
    To resume interpersonal relationships and be successful in dealing with day-to-day events

LONG-TERM PSYCHOLOGICAL EFFECTS OF SEXUAL ASSAULT

Integration/resolution phase - Time period: Months—years—never

The resolution/integration phase is the culmination of the previous phases; in this phase the sexual assault experience is integrated into the whole of the victim's life experience. This phase usually occurs when the victim is able to experience anger and focus it on the assailant.

Characteristics:

    Resumption of usual lifestyle OR completion of change in lifestyle.
    Sexual anxiety with gradual return to usual sexual patterns.
    Public reactions to situations reminding victims of the assault.
    Anxiety/depression may be precipitated by seemingly unrelated events.

Areas of concern/fears:

    Depression—usually the result of anger and rage turned inward

Appendix E

Anger, rage, hostility
Shame, self-blame
Control
Guilt
Repetition of the rape, in flashbacks and daydreams; fantasies
Traumatophobia—phobias of similar places or people
Sexuality
Relationships to men
Independence vs. dependence
Why me?

Needs:

To know that the counselor/therapist is knowledgeable about sexual assault
To believe that she/he will improve, i.e. not be in the same psychological state forever
To be reassured that her/his feelings are normal
To feel independent and in control

AMONG THE REASONS GIVEN BY VICTIMS FOR NOT REPORTING RAPE

— The fear of being accused of *participation* (consent);
— The fear of being accused of *provocation* (What were you doing or wearing that provoked him.')
— The fear of being accused of *irresponsibility* ('Why weren't you at home where you belong?')
— The *desire of parents* to prevent publicity, *further ordeal,* or emotional injury to their child;
— The experience of *shame* or a desire to protect her reputation ('Nice girls don't get raped.');
— Fear of *retaliation* by the offender or his friends;
— Fear of the *reaction* of her parents or her husband;
— Fear of *ridicule*;
— A style of life or set of circumstances which may render her story *suspect* (i.e. accepting a 'date' which ends in rape);
— Sentimental *ideological notions* ('Nobody should be in prison.' etc.);
— Fear of police procedures; *fear of appearing in court and testifying*;
— Lack of *information* about actions and social services available to victims;
— The belief that because there are so *few convictions,* it is pointless to report the crime.

Appendix F:
Beware...BE AWARE. NEW YORK POLICE DEPARTMENT

**CHECKLIST FOR
VICTIMS OF SEXUAL ASSAULT**

Report CRIME IMMEDIATELY to the POLICE DEPARTMENT.... DIAL 911.

1. Do not wash or douche.

2. Do not touch, move or destroy any article that may be evidence.

3. Have medical exam and internal gynecological exam at the nearest Hospital Emergency Room, as soon as possible.

 a) Inform doctor of exact acts committed upon you. He should note any medical evidence of them.

 b) Semem smears must be taken by doctor.

 c) Doctor will note any bruises or injuries (bleeding, lacerations, etc.) external or internal.

 d) Doctor should test for venereal diseases and pregnancy later (if relevant).

4. Inform Police Department investigator of ALL details of attack, however intimate, and of anything unusual you may have noted about the attacker. Remember what he said and how he said it. It could lead to his arrest.

5. Show police any external bruises or injuries, however minor, resulting from the attack. Also show injuries to a friend or relative who might be available as a corroborative witness at the trial.

6. Give any clothing that was stained or torn (including undergarments) during the commission of the crime to the Police for analysis.

7. WHEN CALM.... make note of events of attack. This includes unusual details, direction in which you last saw him running, description (height, weight, clothing, type of build, color of skin, hair, facial oddities, scars, jewelry, etc.).

**THE VICTIM IS *NOT* TO BLAME,
THE VICTIMIZER IS.**

**SEX CRIMES REPORT LINE
AVAILABLE 7 DAYS A WEEK, 24 HOURS A DAY
732 - 7706**

BOROUGH SEX CRIMES DETECTIVE SQUADS

Manhattan
(20 Precinct)
120 W. 82 St.   580 - 6436

Brooklyn
(71 Precinct)
421 Empire Blvd.   735 - 0517

Bronx
(48 Precinct)
450 Cross Bronx Expwy.   220 - 5385

Queens
(112 Precinct)
68-40 Austin St.   520 - 9363

Staten Island
(122 Precinct)
2320 Hylan Blvd.   667 - 2250

ROBERT J. McGUIRE   JAMES T. SULLIVAN
Police Commissioner   *Chief of Detectives*

**POLICE DEPARTMENT CITY OF NEW YORK
DETECTIVE BUREAU**

BM 142 (Rev. 1-81 — E.K.)

WOMEN!
... Beware
... Be Aware

(Safeguards Against Sexual Assault)

Appendix F

SEX CRIMES ARE NOT CRIMES OF PASSION. SEX CRIMES ARE CRIMES OF VIOLENCE. FAR FROM BEING IMPULSIVE BEHAVIOR, MOST SEXUAL ASSAULT IS PLANNED. THIS CRIME COULD HAPPEN TO YOU. NO MATTER YOUR AGE, COLOR, WEALTH OR MARITAL STATUS....

BE AWARE ... TAKE PRECAUTIONS

▶ ▶ ▶

At Home

1. If you live alone you should list ONLY your initials and last name in the phone directory and on a mailbox.

2. Be sure to lock your doors, even if you are at home, and even if you only leave for a few minutes (to walk the dog, get the mail, put out the garbage, hang out the laundry, etc.).

3. Shades or blinds should be on every window.

4. If you live in a basement or first floor apartment, bars should be put on the windows by the landlord.

5. NEVER open the door automatically. Require the caller to identify himself/herself satisfactorily (repairpersons, delivery persons, police officers, public servants, etc.). Utilize chain bolt when checking identification.

6. If a stranger asks to use your phone, DO NOT permit him/her to enter. Offer to summon emergency assistance or make the call for that person.

7. Inside and outside lights give you a good deal of protection. Leave lights on at night, even when away from home. Change the location of inside lighting from time to time.

8. Leave light on over door you will be using when you return home after dark. Use timers. Have key READY so that door can be opened immediately.

9. If a window or door has been forced or broken while you were absent, DO NOT ENTER OR CALL OUT. Use a neighbor's phone IMMEDIATELY to call police and wait outside until they arrive.

In Elevators

1. If you live in an apartment where you know the other residents and find yourself in the lobby with a stranger, let that person take the elevator and wait for it to return for you . . . if you are on the elevator and someone gets on whose presence makes you uneasy, get off at the next floor.

ALWAYS STAND NEAR THE CONTROL PANEL.

If threatened, hit the alarm button and press as many of the other buttons as you can reach with your arm, elbow, etc., enabling the door to open at any of several floors.

Walking

1. Whenever possible, AVOID WALKING ALONE AT NIGHT.

2. After getting off a bus or leaving a subway station, LOOK AROUND to see whether you are being followed.

3. If someone suspicious is behind you or ahead of you, cross the street. If necessary, crisscross from one side to another, back and forth. DON'T BE AFRAID TO RUN.

(One of the criminal's greatest assets is his ability to surprise you, to attack when you least expect it. Should you continue to be followed, be prepared to SCREAM AND RUN ....)

4. BE EXTRA AWARE OF WHAT'S AROUND YOU. Walk closer to the curb to avoid passing too close to shrubbery, dark doorways and other places of concealment. Shun shortcuts, especially through backyards, parking lots, and alleyways.

5. If a car approaches you and you are threatened, SCREAM AND RUN in the direction opposite that of the car. (The driver will have to turn around to pursue you.)

6. Dress for mobility. Many styles are nice but make moving harder on you.

7. Try not to overload yourself with packages, books, large purses, etc.

8. Never hitchhike or accept a ride from a stranger.

9. When arriving home by taxi or private auto, request the driver to wait until you are inside.

10. Have your key ready in hand, so your house door can be opened immediately.

Driving

1. When practicable, travel on well lighted, more populated streets and thoroughfares. Keep windows closed and doors locked.

2. Keep your car in gear while halted at traffic "lights" and "signs". If your safety is threatened, hold down on the horn and drive away as soon as possible.

3. Check your rear view mirror. If you believe you are being followed by another car, do not drive into your driveway or park in a deserted area. Pull over to the curb at a spot where there are people, and let the car pass you. If the car continues to follow, drive to the nearest place where you can get help. (Gas station, police station, fire house, etc.)

4. If you should be followed into your driveway, stay in your car with the doors locked until you can identify the occupants or know the driver's intent. Sound horn to get the attention of neighbors or as an effort to scare the other driver off.

5. When parking at night select a place that will be lighted when you return. Check for loiterers before leaving the car.

6. Never leave car keys in the ignition, even if you are only parked for a short time. Take them with you, and make sure that the car is locked.

7. Never pick up a hitchhiker or offer a ride to a stranger. Offer to summon emergency assistance or make a phone call for someone whose auto is apparently disabled. (Stay inside your locked auto when making offer.)

8. Be conscious of your own auto maintenance. If a breakdown occurs, tie a white cloth to the door handle or antenna, wait for P.D. assistance inside your locked auto. If a "good samaritan" offers help (mechanical or otherwise) pass money for an appropriate phone call via your slightly opened window.

9. Don't let your auto's fuel gauge go below "half" before filling the gas tank FOR SAFETY'S SAKE. . . .

Appendix G:
SILENCE FREES A RAPIST TO STRIKE AGAIN! NEWARK POLICE DEPARTMENT

Help SARA Help You!

BREAK THE SILENCE!

Report a rape to SARA IMMEDIATELY after it happens! Any detail you can give to SARA is extremely important since it can help lead to an arrest and conviction.

CALL 733-RAPE

SILENCE FREES A RAPIST To Strike Again!

HELP US HELP YOU! SARA, a special agency in the City of Newark offers sensitive, specialized care to rape victims.

SARA is The Criminal Justice Planning Office of the City of Newark, The Essex County Prosecutor's Office, the Newark Police Department, the United Hospitals of Newark and the Junior League of Montclair-Newark, Incorporated, all working together in a coordinated community effort to reduce sex crimes and to assist sex crime victims in Newark.

101

**SEX ASSAULT
RAPE ANALYSIS UNIT
20 Park Place
Newark, New Jersey**

Whenever a rape goes unreported, a rapist is free to assault another innocent person. Too many women feel guilty and embarrassed after having been raped. Yet, the first step toward recovery from rape begins when a victim reports the crime.

MYTHS ABOUT RAPE:

No one listens to a rape victim. A victim fears she won't be taken seriously or will be humiliated as if she "seduced" the assailant.

Hospitals and doctors won't treat a rape victim.

If I report a rape, then everyone will know.

The police and hospital personnel don't care about rape victims.

The police will never find the rapist, and even if they do, he won't be convicted.

FACTS ABOUT SARA:

SARA offers sensitive, understanding treatment to rape victims and helps them get medical care, information on legal procedures, and counseling services. Police, doctors and nurses treat the victim with respect and dignity. They make no value judgements about the assault.

Rape victims receive emergency medical treatment at United Hospitals in Newark. Treatment to prevent pregnancy and venereal disease is offered to each victim. Confidentiality is maintained at the SARA Unit, in the hospitals, and at the police station. No one breaks this confidentiality. Both male and female personnel have been selected for their sensitivity as well as investigative skills. They are trained in crisis intervention and understand a victims fears and feelings. During SARA's first year of operation, there was an increased reported rate of 66% and a conviction rate of 87%.

What to do in case of sexual assault:

1. Get to a safe place.
2. Call SARA, 733-RAPE.
3. Do not bathe or douche; you will receive medical treatment.
4. Get a medical examination and treatment as soon as possible.
5. Inform police of all details of the assault.
6. Give all stained or torn clothing to the police; undergarments are especially important.

REFERENCES

Adler, Z. (1982) 'The reality of rape trials', *New Society,* 4 February

Amir, M. (1971) *Patterns of forcible rape,* University of Chicago Press, Chicago

Archbold, J. (1982) *Pleading, evidence and practice in criminal cases,* 41st edn, Sweet and Maxwell, London

Bard, M. and Ellison, K. (1974) 'Crisis intervention and the investigation of forcible rape', *The Police Chief,* May

Bard, M. and Sangrey, D. (1979) *The crime victim's book,* Basic Books, New York

Birmingham Rape Crisis Centre (1981) *Report, 1980*

Blair, Ian (1982) *'Rape: a new approach for police',* unpublished report to the Home Office

Bottomley, A.K. and Coleman C.A. (1980) 'Understanding crime rates' in Clarke, R.V.G. and Hough J.M. (eds.), *The effectiveness of policing,* Gower, Farnborough

Brownmiller, S. (1975) *Against our will,* Simon and Schuster, New York

Burgess, A. and Holmstrom, L. (1974) 'Rape trauma syndrome,' *American Journal of Psychiatry,* 121, 9

Center for Women Policy Studies (1974) *Rape and its victims,* Washington, DC

Chambers, G. and Millar, A. (1983) *Investigating sexual assault,* A Scottish Office Social Research Study, HMSO, Edinburgh

Chappell, D., Geis, R. and Geis, G. (1977) *Forcible rape: the crime, the victim and the offender,* Columbia University Press

Chappell, D. and Singer, S. (1977) 'Rape in New York City' in Chappell, D. Geis, R. and Geis, G., *Forcible rape: the crime, the victim and the offender,* Columbia University Press

Chartered Institute of Public Finance and Accountancy (1982) *Police statistics. Estimates, 1982/83,* CIPFA Statistical Information Service, London

Clark, L. and Lewis, D. (1977) *The price of coercive sexuality,* The Women's Press, Toronto

Clifford, B. and Bull, R. (1978) *The psychology of person identification,* Routledge and Kegan Paul, London

Criminal Law Revision Committee (1984) *Fifteenth report. Sexual offences,* Cmnd 9213, HMSO, London

Csida, J. and Csida, J. (1974) *Rape: how to avoid it and what to do about it,* Books for Better Living, Los Angeles

Draper, K. (1983) *The practice of psychosexual medicine,* John Libley, London

Edwards, S. (1981) *Female sexuality and the law,* Martin Robertson, Oxford

Federal Bureau of Investigation (annual) *Uniform crime reports,* US Department of Justice, Washington, DC

Firth, A. (1975) 'Interrogation', *Police Review,* no. 4324, 28 November

Forcible rape (1975-8) Vols. I-XI, National Institute of Law Enforcement and Criminal Justice, US Government Printing Office, Washington, DC

Griffin, S. (1975) 'The all American crime' in Schultz, L. *Rape victimology,* Charles C. Thomas, Illinois

Groth, N. (1978) *Men who rape,* Plenum Press, London

Holmstrom, L. and Burgess, A. (1978) *The victim of rape: institutional reactions,* John Wiley, New York

Home Office (1975) *Report of the advisory group on the law of rape* (Heilbron Report), Cmnd 6352, HMSO, London

—— (1976) *Criminal statistics England and Wales 1975,* Cmnd 6566, HMSO, London

—— (1978) *Judges' rules and administrative directions to the police,* Circular No 89/1978, HMSO, London

—— (1981) *Criminal statistics England and Wales 1980,* Cmnd 8376, HMSO, London

—— (1983a) *Circular No 25/1983 Investigation of offences of rape*

—— (1983b) *Criminal Statistics England and Wales 1982,* Cmnd 9048, HMSO, London

Hough, M. and Mayhew, P. (1983) *The British crime survey,* Home Office Research Study No. 76, HMSO, London

Lindemann, E. (1944) 'Symptomology and management of acute grief', *American Journal of Psychology,* no. 101

London Rape Crisis Centre (1978a) Rape Counselling and Research Project, *Second Annual Report.* London

—— (1978b) *Rape, police and forensic practice,* evidence submitted to the Royal Commission on Criminal Procedure, London

—— (1982) Rape counselling and research project, *Third report.* London

Marsh, J., Geist, A. and Caplan, N. (1982) *Rape and the limits of law reform*, Auburn House, Boston

National Center for the Prevention and Control of Rape (1979) *Grants awarded by the National Centre for the Prevention and Control of Rape: short summaries*

President's Commission on Law Enforcement and Administration of Justice (1967) *The challenge of crime in a free society*, US Government Printing Office, Washington, DC

Queen's Bench Foundation (1975) *Rape victimization study*, San Francisco

Report of the Commissioner of Police of the Metropolis (annual), HMSO, London

Russell, D. (1975) *The politics of rape: the victim's perspective*, Stein and Day, New York

Shapland, J. (1981) 'The victim in the criminal justice system', unpublished report to the Home Office

Shultz, L. (1975) *Rape victimology*, Charles C. Thomas, Illinois

Smart, C. (1976) *Women, crime and criminology. A feminist critique*, Routledge and Kegan Paul, London

Temkin, J. (1982) 'Towards a modern law of rape,' *Modern Law Review*, Vol. 45, no. 4

US Department of Justice (1981) *Criminal victimization in the United States, 1979*, US Government Printing Office, Washington, DC

Walmsley, R. and White, K. (1979) *Sexual offences, consent and sentencing*, Home Office Research Study No. 54, HMSO, London

Weis, K. and Borges, S. (1975) 'Victimology and rape: the case of the legitimate victim' in Schultz, L. (ed.) *Rape victimology*, Charles C. Thomas, Illinois

Wigmore, J. (1970) *Evidence in trials at common law*, Little Brown, Boston

INDEX

Adler, A. 9
Amir, M. 24, 25, 26
Archbold, J. 53
assailants
  ages 16n1
  and police investigators 2
  identification evidence 49-51
  insanity 27
  motivation 27-8
  non-sexual motivation 27
  psychological profiling 50
Association of Police Surgeons (UK) 36, 37-8, 75

Bard, M. 28, 29
Big Dan's Tavern case 8, 39n3
Birmingham Rape Crisis Centre *see* rape crisis centres
Blair, I. 6
Borges, S. 30
Bottomley, A. 61-2
British Crime Survey 6, 52
Brownmiller, S. 7, 21, 53, 54
Bull, R. 51
Burgess, A. 28-30, 36, 65
burn-out 69, 78, 83

Center for Prevention of Rape 21-2
Center for Women Policy Studies 19, 65, 67
Chambers, G. 6, 9, 10n4, 24, 25, 52, 54, 59, 61, 63, 64n1, 68-9, 76-7, 81
Chappell, D. 32, 53
Chartered Institute of Public Finance and Accountancy 53
circumstances of occurrence of rape 24-6
Clark, L. 64n1
clear-up rate *see* detection rate
Clifford, B. 51
Coleman, C. 61-2
consent
  and cultural assumptions 27
  as defence 62-4
  nature of 63
  police training USA 63
  Scottish police view 63
constitutional comparison USA/UK 17-20, 73

corroboration 22, 63
crime recording policy 56-62 *passim*
Criminal Law Revision Committee
  15th Report on Sexual Offences 6, 11-12, 53
criminal statistics
  accuracy of recorded figures USA/UK 13-14; *see also* non-reporting of rape
  difficulty of comparison USA/UK 16, 59-60
crisis theory 26
Csida, J. 26, 54

detection of rape offences
  effect of new approach 16
detection rate
  comparison, specific police departments 60-1
  comparison USA/UK 16
  low and high rates for rape 55-62
  low rate as indicator of efficiency 60-1
detectives
  interaction with suspect 2
  suggested caseload 76-7
  United Kingdom: expertise 2; female 78-9; recommendations for deployment 75-8; squads not recommended 76-7
  United States: division of work 19; hours of work 19; responsibility at crime scenes 19; summary of view of rape 65
  see also rape squads
Director of Public Prosecutions 18-19
disquiet (public) over rape
  comparison USA/UK 8-9
district attorneys
  criteria for prosecution 18; San Francisco Police Department 44
  investigative capacity 18
  relationship with police 18
  role 18
Draper, K. 30

Edwards, S. 9
Ellison, K. 28

Index

enjoyment of rape, myth of 25-6
evidence
  admissibility 20
  anonymity of victims 22
  corroboration 22
  lack of consent 22; *see also* consent
  previous convictions 20
  sexual penetration 22

false reports of rape 53-4
  and legal procedure 53
  police view 54
  proportion 54
  types of falsity 54
Federal Bureau of Investigation
  function 17
Firth, A. 10n4, 54
Forcible rape 7, 24, 31, 32, 34, 49, 56, 67, 76-7
forensic evidence
  comparison USA/UK 48-9

Geis, G. 53
Geis, R. 53
gender of interviewer
  American findings 67
  and psychology of victim 67
  recommendations UK 78-9
Griffin, S. 13
Groth, N. 27-8, 65
Guardsman's case (*R v Holdsworth*) 9

Hale, Lord Chief Justice 55
Hitchhiker's case
  and 'contributory negligence' 9
Holmstrom, L. 28-30, 36, 65
Home Office Circular on Rape (1983) 6, 36
homosexual offences 13
hospitals for victim examination 36-7
Hough, M. 6, 52

identification evidence
  comparison USA/UK 49-50
identification parades 50-1
impossibility of rape, myth of 26
inactivation *see* no-criming
incidence of rape
  accuracy of recorded figures *see* criminal statistics
  comparison USA/UK 13-16
incidence of rape, Metropolitan Police District 14-15
incidence of rape, UK 13-15
incidence of rape, USA 7, 13-15

indecent assaults
  explanation of terminology 12
interview techniques
  and crisis intervention 66-7
  and gender of interviewer 67
  comparison USA/UK 66-9
  location 67
  recommendations for UK 79-81
  timing 68, 79-80

Judges' Rules 20
judicial comparison USA/UK 17-20
jury vetting 20

Kansas Police Department 56-62 *passim*
  crime recording policy 57

Law Enforcement Assistance Administration 21-2
  see also Forcible rape
Lewis, D. 64n1
liaison with non-police bodies, UK
  recommendations 83-5, 88
liaison with non-police bodies, USA 47, 71, 84
Lindemann, E. 28
location of rape offences 24
London Rape Crisis Centre *see* rape crisis centres
Los Angeles Police Department 23, 45-6, 58

Marsh, J. 53
Mayhew, P. 6, 52
media
  and sexual assault 87
medical services for victims USA/UK 36-9, 74-5
medical services UK
  recommendations 74-5
medical services USA
  assistance to investigation 39
  protocol 36-7
  use of hospitals 36-7
  victim as patient 37
Metropolitan Police
  and London Rape Crisis Centre 34-5, 84
  and this study 1, 78, 81
  computerised indices 50
  crisis intervention training 81
  geographic size 77
  identification evidence 50-1
  incidence of rape 14-15

108 *Index*

victim interviews 68-9
Millar, A. 6, 9, 10n4, 24, 25, 52, 54, 59, 61, 63, 64n1, 68-9, 76-7, 81
Miranda Rules 20
modus operandi
 computer systems 50
Morgan, DPP v 9, 11
myths concerning rape 23-8
 circumstances of assault 24-6
 common beliefs 23
 effects on victim 23
 reasons for assault 26-8

Nash, O. 25
National Association of Victims Support Schemes 35-6, 84-5
National Center for the Prevention and Control of Rape 22
new approach
 limits of 1
 rationale for adoption 74
 summary 65, 88
Newark Police Department 40-1, 53, 58, 72
New York Police Department 41-3, 72
 Sex Crimes Analysis Unit 42
no-criming 56-62 *passim*
 proportion of offences UK 59-61
 recommendations 80
non-reporting of rape 51-3
 police policies to counteract 53
 proportion of offences reported 52
 reasons 52-3
 see also criminal statistics

O'Reilly, H. 42-3, 70

personnel *see* gender of interviewer
photographs
 identification by 49-50
plea bargaining 20
Police Bursaries Trust 6
police departments, USA
 diversity of agencies 17-18, 65
 field studies 40-7
 performance against rape 7, 16
 political sensitivity 20
 senior appointments 20
police discretion in investigations 54-5
police forces, UK
 standardisation 17
police interview techniques *see* interview techniques
Police Staff College, Bramshill 5
police surgeons 36-9
 female 38
pregnancy
 fear and treatment of 37-9
President's Commission on Law Enforcement and the Administration of Justice 52
prosecuting authorities
 comparison USA/UK 17-18
 see also district attorneys
publicity, UK
 recommendations 66
publicity, USA
 and police department image 45-6, 71
 for prevention and advice 72

Queen's Bench Foundation 7

rape
 as a matter for women 21
 as a political issue 21-2
 as primarily non-sexual 27-8
 as violence 25-6, 65
rape analysis units
 over-complex suggested 22
 Los Angeles 45-6
 New York 41-2
Rape Counselling and Research Project 9
rape crisis centres 31-6
 and victim support schemes in UK 35-6
 Birmingham 24, 52; relationship with West Midlands Police 34, 83
 locations in UK 92
 London 9, 23, 24, 30, 39n4, 52; relationship with Metropolitan Police 34-5, 83-4
 Los Angeles 31
 origins in USA 31
 purpose 32
 relationship with police in UK 33-4, 85
 relationship with police in USA 32-3
 restrictions on future growth in UK 35, 85
rape squads
 New York Police Department 41-3
 suggestion for all-female rejected 22
 suggestion UK rejected 76-7
rape suspects *see* assailants
rape trauma syndrome 28-31
 and reporting rape 29-30
 and trial 30
 relevance to police 30-1, 65, 70, 81

Index

Rape Treatment Center
  Los Angeles 45-6, 67, 69
reasons for rape 26-8
relationship of offender and victim 24
reporting of rape
  effect on victim 30
resistance and social ritual 27
resistance in rape 25
responsibility of victim, myth of 26-7
Russell, D. 7, 32

San Fransisco Police Department 43-5
  crime recording policy 56, 58, 60-1
Sangrey, D. 29
Schultz, L. 52
sex of interviewer *see* gender of
  interviewer
Sexual Offences Act (1956)
  provisions 11
Sexual Offences (Amendment) Act
  (1976) 11, 22
Sexual Trauma Service
  San Fransisco 37, 44-5, 52, 67, 70, 94, 95-8
Shapland, J. 9, 39n4
Singer, S. 32
Smart, C. 9
social developments
  comparison USA/UK 7-8, 87-8
Solicitor General for Scotland
  resigns over rape prosecution 9
spousal rape 12-13
  and Australian law 13
  and Scottish law 12
  and USA law 12
stranger rape 24
study of rape
  amount of grants, US 21
Survivor 23, 31, 45, 66, 91-2
suspects *see* assailants

Temkin, J. 53
Thames Valley Police
  rape units 9
time of rape offences 76
training for police, UK
  detectives 81-2
  general recommendations 81-3
  recruits 81
  supervisors 83
training for police, USA 69-70
  John Jay College 70

venereal disease
  fear and treatment of 37-9
verdicts, unanimity 20
victim
  behaviour after rape 29
  myth of enjoyment of rape 25-6
  myth of responsibility for rape 26-7
  reaction to rape 29; *see also* rape
    trauma syndrome
  relationship with offender 24
  resistance 25
  rights in law enforcement 66
victim-precipitated rape 26
victims support schemes 35-6, 84-5
violence in rape 25
  see also rape as violence

Walmsley, R. 9
Weis, K. 30
West Midlands Police 34, 83
White, K. 9
Wigmore, J. 53
withdrawal of complaints 56-62 *passim*
  effect on police efficiency 58
  effects on victim 57-8
  recommendations UK 80
women police, UK 78-9
women's movement, USA
  rise of 7, 21